Studies in Political Science
and Sociology

UNIVERSITY OF PENNSYLVANIA
BICENTENNIAL CONFERENCE

Studies in Political
Science and Sociology

By

HU SHIH
NEWTON EDWARDS
MARK A. MAY
WILLIAM G. CARR
WILLIAM E. RAPPARD
ARTHUR C. COLE
LOUIS WIRTH
CARL KELSEY
ALVIN S. JOHNSON
PHILIP E. MOSELY
WILLIAM HABER

KENNIKAT PRESS, INC./PORT WASHINGTON, N. Y.

UNIVERSITY OF PENNSYLVANIA BICENTENNIAL CONFERENCE
STUDIES IN POLITICAL SCIENCE AND SOCIOLOGY

Copyright 1941 by University of Pennsylvania Press
Reissued 1969 by Kennikat Press by arrangement

Library of Congress Catalog Card No: 68-26201
Manufactured in the United States of America

ESSAY AND GENERAL LITERATURE INDEX REPRINT SERIES

Contents

Contents

Instrumentalism as a Political Concept

By

HU SHIH, Ph.D., Litt.D., L.H.D., LL.D., D.C.L.*

IT HAS always been a great disappointment to me that the movement of pragmatism in all its phases—the greatest and most significant philosophical movement, which has actually spanned a period of over sixty years—has not produced a political philosophy. The purpose of this paper is to suggest a possible pragmatic political theory more or less along the line of the Instrumentalist theory of logic which regards ideas and theories not as final truths but only as hypotheses or intellectual tools to be tested by their consequences.

I shall begin with what may be considered as a common sense view that political institutions—the laws, government, the state—are instrumentalities devised by men for the realization of definite human ends.

Man, whom Bergson calls *Homo Faber*, the tool-making animal, makes all kinds of tools for the performance of all kinds of acts and for the attainment of all kinds of ends. A tool, from the crudest artifact of the Stone Age to the most complex piece of modern machinery, is a means for attaining an anticipated end. Every tool implies two essential elements: first, an idea of the way or the means to realize the end in view, and secondly, the embodiment of that idea in some material, practical form. A tool is good when it can attain the anticipated end satisfactorily; it is often revised and improved as human ingenuity can find ways to make it function more effectively; it is discarded only when it can no longer perform the task required of it or when a better and more efficient tool can be devised to take its place.

Social and political institutions are tools in the same sense: they are instrumentalities more or less consciously devised for the achievement of more or less consciously conceived ends. The judge, the king, the laws, the government, the state, are

* Chinese Ambassador to the United States.

1

just such tools invented and evolved by man for the purpose of realizing ends which cannot be satisfactorily realized by private and separate individuals. As instruments for definite ends, they, too, are to be judged, appraised or condemned according as they succeed or fail in realizing the intended or desired ends.

It is comparatively easy to see that laws, from the most ancient laws of Hammurabi and Moses down to the laws and constitutions of our own day, have certainly been consciously devised instrumentalities for the purpose of attaining definite human ends. Even the primitive and archaic polities may also be considered as deliberately formed instrumentalities for realizing definite ends—even though the ends may have been the perpetuation of certain religious beliefs and practices or the common defense against a threatening enemy tribe.

Naturally, the modern states and governments that have been formed or reformed in the last three hundred years, under written and published constitutions, are the best illustrations of the Instrumentalist view of political institutions. One may even be tempted to suggest that some form of Instrumentalist view of institutions has always been the political philosophy, avowed or unconscious, of the political reformers and the democratic movements of the last three hundred years.

The Declaration of Independence of 1776 lays down as a self-evident truth the principle that governments are instituted for a definite purpose, and that, "whenever any Form of Government becomes destructive of these ends, it is the Right of the People to alter or to abolish it, and to institute a new Government." The Constitution of 1787 revises and broadens these "ends" in its Preamble:—

We, the People of the United States, in order to form a more perfect union, establish Justice, insure domestic Tranquillity, provide for the common defence, promote the general Welfare, and secure the Blessings of Liberty to ourselves and our Posterity, do ordain and establish this Constitution for the United States of America.

The founding fathers of the American republic, indeed, were fully conscious that they were doing something which had never been done before by mankind with so much freedom and so much deliberation, namely, the deliberate creation of governments and states. "Our Revolution," says Thomas Jefferson, "presented us an album on which we were free to write what we pleased." And Thomas Paine expressed the same feeling even more emphatically when he declared: "We are brought at once to the point of seeing Government begin, as if we had lived in the beginning of time." Consciously to define the ends of government and deliberately devise the structure of government best calculated to achieve them—that is political Instrumentalism.

In the works of English Utilitarians or Philosophical Radicals of the last century, we often find expressions of this Instrumentalist view of political institutions. A very remarkable formulation of this view is contained in the opening paragraphs of the first chapter of John Stuart Mill's "Considerations on Representative Government." According to this theory, says Mill, "government is conceived as strictly a practical art, giving rise to no questions but those of means to an end. Forms of government are assimilated to any other expedients for the attainment of human objects. They are regarded as wholly an affair of invention and contrivance. Being made by man, it is assumed that man has the choice either to make them or not, and how or on what pattern they shall be made. Government, according to this conception, is a problem to be worked like any other question of business. The first step is to define the purposes which governments are required to promote. The next is to inquire what form of government is best fitted to fulfil those purposes. Having satisfied ourselves on these two points, and ascertained the form of government which combines the greatest amount of good with the least of evil, what further remains is to obtain the concurrence of our countrymen—in the opinion which we have privately arrived at. To find the best form of government; to persuade others that it is the best; and having done so, to stir them up to insist on having it, is the order of ideas in the minds of those who adopt this view of political philosophy. They look upon a constitution in the same light (difference of scale being allowed for) as they would upon a steam plough or a threshing machine."

Early in 1916, Dr. John Dewey published two essays entitled "Force, Violence and Law" and "Force and Coercion." In these now much-neglected essays, Dewey developed an Instru-

mentalistic theory of law on the basis of an Instrumentalistic
theory of force. Dewey points out that

force figures in different rôles. Sometimes it is energy; sometimes it is
coercion or constraint; sometimes it is violence. Energy is power
used with a eulogistic meaning; it is power of doing work, har-
nessed to accomplishment of ends. But it is force none the less—
brute force, if you please, and rationalized only by its results.
Exactly the same force running wild is called violence. The objection to violence is not that it involves the use of force, but that it is
a waste of force; that it uses force idly or destructively. . . . Energy
becomes violence when it defeats or frustrates purpose instead of
executing or realizing it. When the dynamic charge blows up human
beings instead of rocks, when its outcome is waste instead of production, destruction instead of construction, we call it not energy
or power but violence. . . .
Law is a statement of the conditions of the organization of energies
which, when unorganized, would conflict and result in violence—
that is, destruction or waste. . . . What is called law may always,
I suggest, be looked at as describing a method for employing force
economically, efficiently, so as to get results with the least waste. . . .
No ends are accomplished without the use of force. It is consequently no presumption against a measure, political, international,
jural, economic, that it involves a use of force. But [here Dewey
stresses his Instrumentalist philosophy] antecedent and abstract
principles can not be assigned to justify the use of force. The cri-
terion of value lies in the relative efficiency and economy of the
expenditure of force as a means to an end.

Dewey's Instrumentalistic theory of force brings out in prominent relief one phase of political institutions which has often
been neglected by most liberals and radicals, namely, the active
power or force necessary for the working of these institutions.
No tool can act by itself. An instrument, as a means to an end,
in its complete sense, must include the power required to make
it work, as well as the device or machinery for harnessing that
power to act in a definite manner or direction in order to attain the desired end. Ends therefore are achieved only by
adequate energy being properly controlled and directed
through well devised machinery. Both the machinery and the
power are essential and integral parts of the effective working
instrumentality. Law, as formulation of the conditions for the
use of force, is only a necessary condition for the successful
harnessing of the energies for a desirable end. To harness

energy for the accomplishing of certain ends, is necessarily co-ercive—just as coercive as the red traffic light bringing all traffic to a sudden stop. But because of the efficiency in achiev-ing the ends, such constraint is usually eulogized and willingly borne.

In the same Instrumentalistic sense, we may regard govern-ment as the public agency or sum of public agencies for the realization of definite public ends by the use of organized ener-gies or forces. Constitutional government or government by law is the government under which the conditions for the use of its forces are definitely formulated and effectively enforced. Authoritarian or dictatorial government is one wherein such formulation is either lacking or, when present in the statute books, cannot be enforced.

A few corollaries may be summarily stated here:

First, this political philosophy of instrumentalism encour-ages intelligent planning and experimentation in government, and furnishes the rational ground for peaceful reform and re-vision. Laws and policies of governments, however wisely for-mulated, are never intended for all times. As new needs and problems of associated life continue to come up and as old ob-jectives expand in their scope or change in their emphasis, the political instrumentalities must needs be modified or reformed from time to time in order that they may continue to serve efficiently and economically the needs of the changing times. A political institution that resists intelligent experimentation and peaceful revision tends to inefficiency, waste, suffering, and violence in reaction.

In the second place, this Instrumentalistic view of political institutions gives us what may be regarded as the most reason-able and scientific justification for democratic control of the governmental machinery. The political machine, the greatest and most powerful machine ever invented and handled by the intelligence of man, can most easily get out of control and run wild. It needs constant attention, jealous vigilance, and intelli-gent direction and control. All the checks and controls which the political genius and experience of man have invented for the purpose of safeguarding the machinery of the state against the dangers of abuse, corruption, despotism, are the political brakes, gears, and safety valves without which the monstrous

Leviathan might run amok and cause tremendous damage, violence and destruction.

In the third place, the political instrumentalities can be more fully and more positively used for the benefit of man, so long as they are subject to the safeguards of democratic control. The danger of a machine lies not in the stupendous amount of power it generates, but in the weakness of its controls—its brakes and safety-valves. The despotism of the totalitarian systems does not lie in the great power wielded by the government, but in the total absence of methods and means of controlling that power and checking its abuse. With effective and conscious methods of democratic control, a modern government machinery can greatly enhance its positive usefulness and efficacy without the danger of becoming despotic and dictatorial.

The greatest positive contribution of the Anglo-Saxon peoples to the political thinking of the world, it seems to me, lies not merely in its traditional emphasis on the problem of democratic control of the machinery of the state, but chiefly in their successful solution of it. No other people in history has succeeded in devising a workable system for the effective control of the machinery of the state. The Anglo-Saxon political evolution and the Anglo-Saxon political thinking have combined to produce more than one system of democratic control, under which powerful safeguards are provided for keeping governmental power within the control of the governed. In countries with such well-developed traditions and institutions of democratic control, the time seems to be ripe for the development of a more positive political philosophy with proper appreciation of the instrumental function of the state as well as due emphasis on the importance of intelligent direction, experimentation, and criticism of its functioning. Government is a tool for us to use, to experiment with, to master and control, to love and cherish, but not something to be afraid of. A government intelligently conscious of its own instrumental potentialities, and, at the same time, subject to democratic control, is the only kind of political machinery worthy of the new age of science and technology.

The Evolution of American Educational Ideals

NEWTON EDWARDS, Ph.D.*

THE men who came to Virginia with Captain John Smith and
to Massachusetts with Governor John Winthrop brought with
them the heritage of a long-established culture. Their notions
with respect to law and government, religion, economic organization, social classification and education were notions enter-
tained by one group or another of the Englishmen who made
up seventeenth-century England. It is not strange, therefore,
that new-world institutions were cast in old-world molds, that
the essential elements of an old social order were woven into
the very fabric of American life. But European ideas, values,
and traditions could not for long remain unaffected by the influence of environment. As each succeeding generation of
Americans pushed deeper into the shadows of the wilderness,
old ties with Europe were loosened, institutional forms were
changed, and a new society emerged, more democratic than
the old and with purposes and ideals distinctly its own.

Much has transpired in America since the early colonists
landed at Jamestown and Plymouth. As men have wrought
and toiled in isolation or together on farm and in factory to
develop a continent, to lay the basis and erect the structure of
a great industrial civilization, they have formed and reformed
their essential social institutions, they have defined and rede-
fined those human values which determine the quality of individual living. Each succeeding generation has contributed
some new element to the design of American life. From time
to time shifts have occurred in the locus of political and economic power, in the ideology underpinning the state, in the
structure of the economy, and in the arrangement of social
classes. And since education is always anchored in the

* Professor of Education, University of Chicago.

7

civilization of which it is a part, American educational ideals
have constantly reflected the ideals and purposes of the social
order in which they have developed. It is not easy, therefore,
to speak with certainty and precision about American educational ideals; they have varied from time to time, from place
to place, and among the different social classes. But despite
change and diversity certain ideals can be identified and their
origin and development traced with reasonable certainty.

EQUALITY OF EDUCATIONAL OPPORTUNITY

For a hundred and fifty years and more the development of
American education was profoundly influenced by the class
structure of society. Englishmen who set sail for America in
the seventeenth century had grown up in a society characterized by sharp class distinctions. Most of them belonged to the
middle and lower classes, but they accepted without serious
question the prevailing system of social classification. It was
not their purpose to establish in America a democratic society.
They hoped rather to improve their personal fortunes within
the general framework of the old order. In America, as in old
England, members of a superior social class—magistrates, the
clergy, and men of means—controlled the government and
shaped public and social policy pretty much to their own ends.
In early America there was little equalitarianism, and this
was as true of education as of government. Even in New England few outstanding leaders looked with favor on democracy
in any form. John Winthrop, the most influential political
figure in early Massachusetts, and John Cotton, the spiritual
leader of the young colony, were both agreed in their dislike
of democracy. Winthrop regarded it as the "meanest & worst
of all formes of Governm't" and Cotton wrote: "Democracy,
I do not conceyve that ever God did ordeyne as a fit government eyther for church or commonwealth. If the people be
governors, who shall be governed?" And the ruling class of
magistrates, ministers, and merchants were as jealous of social
status as of political power; they were as bent upon maintaining a due subordination of social rank as upon enforcing a con-
formity of religious belief. They employed all the devices at
their command to maintain their social status. Repeatedly
laws were passed to keep the wages of artisans and laborers

down. The title of "gentleman" or "mister" was reserved for those of superior social position. In the church on the Sabbath morning each must take his place in his accustomed pew which was assigned on the basis of social status. Infinite were the committee meetings to appraise the official position, the wealth, and the age of the various inhabitants of the town in order that all might be seated in the proper order of preference. Class distinctions were also carried into the matter of dress; the function of clothes was not alone to hide one's nakedness and to keep one warm but to reveal the social class to which one belonged. When social underlings began to dress like gentlemen and ladies, to wear silver lace and silken hose, the upper crust became alarmed and promptly took legal measures to arrest this tendency to disturb the well-ordered ranks of society.

It is true, of course, that the New England colonies established systems of public schools, but it must not be supposed that New England leadership in the early days was motivated by the ideal of equality of opportunity. The men responsible for the enactment of the educational legislation in early New England would have stood aghast had they thought that they were promoting the interests of a democratic society. They had the acumen to see that education could be made a vital force in socializing youth in terms of the core values of society, but the kind of society they visualized was not to be characterized by equality of opportunity. One misses the deeper significance of the educational legislation of early New England unless one keeps in mind the whole system of laws which was employed to support the existing scheme of religious, political, economic, and social arrangements, laws designed to regulate practically every aspect of life, private and public, spiritual and material.

Fortunately, magistrates and ministers, merchants and planters, whether in New England, the Middle Colonies, or the South, were not to be the architects of the ultimate design of American society. Gradually power—economic, political, and social—trickled down from the upper crust to the common man, to the yeomen and artisans who built their homes along the elm-shaded streets of New England towns, to the farmers of New York, Pennsylvania, and the back country of the South. Tilling their own acres with their own hands and with the help of their numerous offspring, or performing their daily tasks as carpenters, blacksmiths, tailors, or bricklayers, this middle class was not only the most numerous but in many respects the most important element in American society. Self-respecting, industrious, and ambitious, these middle-class farmers and artisans were able to achieve an economic well-being unrivaled by the middle classes of Europe, and many of them succeeded in amassing enough wealth to enable them to vote and hold public office once suffrage qualifications were put on a property basis. Most important of all, perhaps, they were not ashamed to work with their hands, and they gave to labor a dignity it had not known before. This middle class with its insistence upon the recognition of its importance and its rights was an unwelcome and perhaps unexpected intruder into the social order planned by the founders; it was destined to give American life its essentially democratic character. It was in the minds and hearts of these yeomen and artisans, pioneers in both a physical and spiritual sense, that the great American Dream took form, the vision of a land of equal opportunity for all.

The words of the Declaration of Independence proclaiming that all men are created free and equal must have had a familiar sound to Jefferson's neighbors in back-country Virginia and indeed to men in the back country all the way from Maine to Georgia. And the Revolution which followed was much more than a revolt against England; it was a revolution within a revolution as well. The cause of America against England was also the cause of western farmers against eastern planters and merchants. The men who stuck with Washington at Valley Forge or who charged the heights at King's Mountain were fighting for independence from England; they were also fighting for that way of life towards which the words of the Declaration of Independence pointed.

When the war was over and the new nation established, Jefferson and his followers undertook to give some reality to the high ideal that men are created free and equal. But another generation was to pass before the ideal of equal opportunity was to become the touchstone of statecraft and indeed of all public policy, before it was to ring in unmistakable tones through the thought of the age. If men were in fact to be equal in government, in the economy, and in the intellectual life of the nation, schools, it was firmly believed, must be established with doors equally open to all. Horace Mann proclaimed, and by and large the nation accepted his leadership, that above all devices of human origin education is the great equalizer of the condition of men.

As a people, we have accepted the ideal of equal educational opportunity, but we have never fully understood the wide sweep of its implications. Certainly the gulf that separates the ideal from its realization is wide and there are signs that it may be growing wider. Perhaps the most devastating criticism that can be directed against the American educational system is its widespread failure to provide reasonably equal educational opportunity. In communities where the birth rate is low and the educational load light, where economic resources are the most abundant, where planes of living are high, where the home has most to contribute to cultural and intellectual development, we support education liberally. In communities where the birth rate is high and the burden of child care and nurture disproportionately heavy, where the resource structure is weak, where planes of living are low, and where the cultural-intellectual status of parents is the lowest, we support education inadequately although with great effort. Education can be made a force to equalize the condition of men; it is no less true that it can become a force to create class, race, and regional distinctions. If formal educational attainments condition entrance to some economic and social spheres, and if great opportunities for educational advance are open to some groups while the educational facilities for others remain meager, it is obvious that education becomes an instrument of social stratification and of regional and racial inequality. If in the lives of some children the educational ladders rise high and in the lives of others they scarcely rise at all, the schools may function as a mechanism of social differentiation. The evidence indicates clearly that continuance of present policies creates grave danger that our schools, which we have hitherto regarded as the bulwark of democracy, may in fact become an instrument for creating those very inequalities they were designed to prevent.

SOCIAL MOBILITY

For more than a hundred years the American people have had an abiding faith in education as a means of promoting social mobility, of maintaining a society essentially free from class and caste. This ideal is even older than that of equal educational opportunity for all with which it is so closely associated. One meets it in its nascent form in the relatively low costs of education in Harvard College in the early days, in the private gifts to Latin schools in New England, and in the numerous endowed schools of colonial South Carolina. Jefferson gave concrete expression to it in his plan for education in Virginia, and it was fostered by the social ideals of the more or less classless society of each succeeding west. In time, social mobility came to be of the essence of American democracy; the way to place and power, so it was felt, should be open to youth of ability and energy regardless of inheritance. Indeed, place and power should, in great degree, be redistributed at the end of each generation.

Modern sociologists are beginning to give us a detailed delineation, an anatomy as it were, of the class and caste structure of present-day society. But historians have long been aware of the "upper uppers" and the "lower lowers" and of at least some of the difficulties that have beset the individual as he has attempted to pass from one class to another. And American parents have not been insensitive to the hazards their offspring would encounter in trying to climb the ladder of opportunity; they have believed with almost a religious zeal that in some way the doors to economic advance and social preferment would open more easily and wider to those with the greatest amount of schooling. The liberality with which the American people have supported their educational institutions reflects as little else does their belief in social mobility as a desirable social goal and their faith in education as a means of enabling each individual to achieve to the full limits of his capacity.

The economic and social forces in American life which gave vitality to the ideal of equal opportunity in a mobile society are losing much of their old vigor. In fact, these are forces which appear to be carrying us in the opposite direction. Cheap land, or land for the taking, was a powerful factor in producing both the ideal and to some extent the reality of a classless society. But now conditions are reversed; agriculture no longer affords expanding employment opportunity for millions of youth. Due to high birth rates among farm women, technological advance, the decline in the rate of population growth, the decline in foreign markets, and other factors, agriculture is able to give employment to only a small fraction of the youth now being dammed up on farms. Gone is Jefferson's dream of a nation of free and independent farmers working the soil they own. Forty-two percent of the farmers of the country are tenants or croppers. Today farmers have an equity of only 39 percent in the land they work. To most farm youth, land ownership appears to be a receding goal. Truly things have changed. Nor is the tendency towards social stratification limited to the farm population; it appears to be spreading into practically every segment of American life.

Faith in social mobility through education has profoundly affected both the quantity and quality of schooling afforded American youth. Since the avenues to places of leadership and prestige, to wealth and power, have most commonly led through the upper reaches of our educational system, the greater part of our educational program has been designed to benefit the few who possessed the qualities necessary to enable them to move up the ladder of opportunity. For those not possessing such qualities, the educational program might have been more vital had it been motivated by the ideal of social adjustment rather than social mobility. At any rate, the question is being raised in some quarters whether the school should not attempt to identify youth who are not likely to reach the upper rungs of the ladder of opportunity and devise for them a program of education which will enable them to do a better job of living where they are. This question poses a challenge to one of America's oldest educational ideals.

EDUCATION AND THE PUBLIC INTEREST

The American people have not, however, regarded the fruits of education as wholly personal and private; from the very beginning education has been vested with a public interest. Although the builders of early New England, with few exceptions, looked with disfavor upon democracy in both church and commonwealth, they did recognize that "the good education of children is of singular behoof and benefit to any commonwealth," whether the commonwealth be democratic or otherwise. To New England, and to Massachusetts in particular, goes the credit of putting this principle into practice and of bequeathing it to future generations. It became fundamental in the New England tradition that every well-ordered state should have its system of public schools. As time passed and the state threw off clerical control and itself became democratic, the old principle in a new setting became a dynamic force in the development of American democracy, both political and cultural.

In the early days of the Republic, the men who were laying the foundation of the American political structure were genuinely afraid that their experiment in free political institutions would fail, and they had no doubt that it would fail if the state neglected to cultivate in youth that degree of social understanding necessary to pass intelligent judgment on public issues. No one familiar with the record can doubt that the dynamics of public education in this country is to be found in the emergence of the democratic state as a form of political organization. The essentially civic character of American education is amply documented in the writings of statesmen and publicists, in the debates of constitutional conventions, in the official pronouncements of organized labor, in editorial opinion, and in numerous court decisions. Repeatedly the courts have been called upon to define the functions of the school in American society; of necessity they have formulated a theory of education based upon what are deemed to be fundamental principles of social policy. In legal theory, public education is essentially and intrinsically a function of government; it is even more, it is an attribute of government. In the democratic state an enlightened citizenry is so essential to the promotion of the public welfare that the maintenance of a system of public education has been regarded as much an attribute of government as the police power, the power to tax, to administer justice, or to maintain military forces. The state's authority to levy taxes for the maintenance of a system of public education has rested primarily on its duty and obligation to promote the general welfare, the good order, and the peace of society.

It has long been fundamental in the American tradition that the very life of the democratic state is at stake in its program of civic education. At times, perhaps most of the time, this program has been inadequate, but the ideal has remained. And as the problems of public policy become increasingly numerous and complex, it is clear that if the youth of this and the next generation are to make democracy work, if they are to meet their responsibility for the successful operation of the national economy and for the advancement of the common culture, they will have to cultivate a greater breadth and comprehensiveness of thought and arrive at a more thorough understanding of the workings of our political, economic, and social arrangements than their elders have ever done.

EDUCATION AS THE GUARDIAN OF "THE FUNDED CAPITAL OF HUMAN EXPERIENCE"

In America education has had a center of interest quite apart from the currents of contemporary political and social change; from the very beginning school and college have been regarded as the special guardians of those accumulations of ideas, knowledge, values, appreciations, and techniques which constitute the capital of human experience. Luckily, the genius of New England early found its fullest expression in the cultivation of the intellectual life. And although the broad humanism of the early Renaissance did not thrive in the fierce heat of religious controversy in a frontier society, it is true that New England leadership kept the flame of humanism from being extinguished entirely. The classical tradition in America at least kept alive the belief that man cannot cut himself away from his culture without deadly peril, that education is concerned with the maintenance and the enrichment of civilization. It has been a fundamental ideal in American education that the experience of the race should be freely accessible to all who may care to profit by it, that no forbidden signs be placed along the avenues that lead through all the reaches and depths of human experience, that freedom of inquiry and expression be cherished and guarded as a priceless heritage. However much men may have differed about those aspects of human experience that were of most worth, the school has always faced the responsibility of identifying those elements in human experience which were in fact the essential elements of the common culture and of organizing them into an effective educational program. Emphasis upon the present and contemporary is always important, and doubly so when the contemporary is pregnant with crisis, but the American people have never for long lost sight of the ideal that education is also concerned with enduring values. And they have not surrendered to the possessors of political and economic power the determination of what those values are.

FREEDOM OF INQUIRY AND THE QUEST FOR KNOWLEDGE

Thomas Jefferson once exclaimed, "I have sworn upon the alter [sic] of God eternal hostility against every form of tyranny over the mind of man." And in a letter to George Ticknor he wrote: "Knowledge is power, knowledge is safety . . . knowledge is happiness." In their determination to free the human intellect from all forms of tyranny and in their faith in knowledge as a means of social progress, Jefferson and his followers were, of course, reflecting the spirit of the Enlightenment.

The remarkable advances in science during the seventeenth and eighteenth centuries changed fundamentally the thought pattern of the age. Men always seek to establish a value pattern, a body of principles which will serve as a touchstone for their thought and action. The eighteenth century saw the exaltation of reason; men sought to find in science the basic principles of human nature, of society, and of the universe itself. Reason was to be the touchstone of all institutions and values. The idea of progress now became a dynamic force; man and his institutions were regarded as capable of almost indefinite perfectibility. If reason and science could be made a basis of human action, so it was thought, old abuses and injustices in church and state and in society generally would be removed. In the early days of the Republic, liberals everywhere looked to education as a means of realizing the ideals of the Enlightenment.

As the years have passed, we have lost some of the earlier enthusiasm for man as a rational animal and it has appeared that science alone cannot be relied on to shape and fashion human institutions. But even so, education has not been relieved of the responsibility of freeing men's minds, of the quest for knowledge, and of assuming an important rôle in the processes of social change. The common man in America has looked to education as a means of improving the economic and social position of the individual; he has also had an abiding faith in education as a means of social progress. And this faith in education as a means of social direction and control has led to a freedom of inquiry which is one of America's most cherished educational ideals.

Failure to realize ideals is a characteristic of both individuals and peoples. However much accomplishment may have fallen short of purpose, the American people have striven for equal educational opportunity; they have shaped educational policy to make it contribute to social mobility; they have thought of education as serving the public interest; they have looked to schools and colleges as the preservers of those enduring values which emerge from human experience; they have regarded education as an indispensable means of social progress; and, to a remarkable degree, they have subsidized the quest for knowledge and guaranteed freedom of inquiry. Even when due allowance is made for failures and defeats—and they have been many—it appears that as a people we have set our face along the path that leads to an all-inclusive cultural democracy. The schools and colleges we have established and maintained have been symbols of our faith that we can solve the problems of human living through trained intelligence without resort to the dictates of arbitrary power.

Falling Short of the Democratic Ideals in Education

By

MARK A. MAY, Ph.D.*

THE recent challenge to democracy by the totalitarian powers has stimulated educators to state more precisely the democratic ideals of education and to inquire to what extent they are being realized. The various committees, commissions, and individuals who have attempted to formulate statements about the aims and functions of education in a democracy seem to agree on two essential points. First, a democratic society is obligated to provide for its youth the amount and kind of education that will enable all individuals to acquire a common body of knowledge and skill that is necessary for effective social living, and that will further provide an opportunity for each to develop his particular native talents. Second, a democracy is obligated to provide an opportunity for each of its citizens to find a position in which he can best serve society with the greatest satisfaction to himself. These two ideals may be stated briefly thus: (1) education for each according to his talents; (2) an occupation for each according to his education.

All who are familiar with the process and the products of the American system of education will agree that we have fallen short of these ideals. Everyone knows that educational opportunities in the common branches are not equally distributed throughout the population, and that special training for the talented is haphazard and fortuitous. Moreover, it is known that only a small fraction of American youth are able to use whatever special training may have been received in school in the occupations which they are destined to enter. We are not generally aware, however, of how far short of our democratic ideals we are actually falling.

* Professor of Educational Psychology and Director, Institute of Human Relations, Yale University.

The various studies and surveys made by the American Youth Commission, the research division of the National Education Association, the United States Office of Education, the President's Commission on Vocational Education, various state and regional groups and especially the New York State Regents' Inquiry, all add up to the general conclusion that the amount and kind of education that American youth of today are actually receiving depend primarily on where they happen to live, the racial or ethnic group to which they belong, and the socio-economic status of the homes from which they come. Educational opportunities are distributed according to native talents or intelligence only to the extent to which they are correlated with these geographic, social, and economic factors. It is probably true that talent is more concentrated in the favored environments and that it is therefore to be expected that educational opportunities would be greatest there, but it is also true that there is an undetermined amount of talent among the underprivileged which the system of public education in a democracy should surely seek out and develop. However, the facts indicate that much of this talent is wasted due to the fact that educational opportunities are distributed according to place of residence, racial groupings, and socio-economic status.

There can be no doubt about the unequal geographic distribution of educational opportunities to the youth of our nation. These inequalities are partly between sections or regions of the Nation—as between rural and urban, urban and suburban, and between counties within a state; they are also partly local—as between one school and another in the same system or in the same community. The differences are apparent mainly in length of school year, buildings and physical facilities, salaries and training of teachers, size of classes, amount of guidance, textbooks, diversity of curriculum, but most of all in the viewpoint and educational philosophy of the school authorities. Communities also vary in the kind of schools provided. Some provide only elementary schools; most have also a general high school; some provide commercial, trade, technical, or agricultural schools; some, junior colleges; and some, municipal or state universities. It is obvious that the amount and kind of schooling that youth receives depend on the quality and type of school he attends and that, in turn, depends to

some degree on where—in what section of the country or of
the state or of the city—the school is located. If a youth lives
on a farm in one of the southern states, the chances are that
his school term will be relatively shorter, that his teachers will
be relatively less well trained or well paid, that the curriculum
of the high school will be less diversified and adapted to individual needs than would be the case if he were living in a
northern city. The best schools of the nation are to be found
in the best residential suburban sections of the larger cities,
or in smaller but relatively wealthy and progressive towns; the
poorest schools are found in the rural areas of the south and
southwest and in the more congested areas of some of the larger
cities.

The best educational opportunities are provided in places
where there are relatively few children in proportion to the
population and where there is high per capita wealth. It appears that the greater the ratio of children to the population
of a section, the less the financial ability to support schools.
For example, Newton Edwards has estimated that the northwestern area of the United States has 30 percent of the nation's
children and 43 percent of the nation's wealth; whereas the
southeastern states have 10 percent of the nation's wealth and
24 percent of the nation's children. "The responsibility for the
care and education of 31% of the nation's children of school
age falls on the farm population, but farmers receive only 9%
of the national income."[1]

This inequality in the geographic distribution of educational
opportunity is dramatically illustrated by Mr. Farnsworth
Crowder, who quotes the following passages from a letter of a
fourteen-year-old Midwestern girl to a friend:

Last year we thought we were hard up because school closed
April first. This year I guess we aren't going to have school at all.
. . . I guess I'll have to give up my plan to take high school, with
the school closed. I feel like crying every time I see it with the doors
and windows boarded up. . . . Do you think you could get on
without a school or even a set of books? Grace has the arithmetic VIII
and I have the grammar. . . . For all of us that go to the parsonage
there is one history book. . . . It stops before the war but I guess

[1] Newton Edwards, *Equal Educational Opportunity for Youth.* A report to the
American Youth Commission, Washington, D. C. American Council on Education, 1939. p. 85.

there hasn't been much since then but trouble and I don't need a book to learn about that.[2]

A second factor that determines the amount and kind of schooling (especially secondary and higher) that American youth receive is the racial or ethnic group to which they belong. This inequality is perhaps most marked in the case of the Negro. In the elementary schools of the nation the proportion of white and Negro children of school age who are in attendance is almost equal. The inequalities appear in the upper levels. The 1930 census shows that of the youth sixteen and seventeen years old, 48 percent of the Negro and 60 percent of the white youth were in school; but of ages eighteen to twenty, 10 percent of the Negroes and 27 percent of the whites were in school. In the Youth Commission's Survey of Maryland, 15 percent of all youth studied were Negroes, only 9 percent of whom were in schools. Two-thirds of the white youth as against one-third of the Negro youth had completed the eighth grade before dropping out. And, further, 30 percent of the whites against 8 percent of the Negroes graduated from high school. Of the Negro youth who attended high school most of them took a vocational, trade, or agricultural course, and relatively few took the college preparatory course. This is in part due to the fact that in the southern states where the whites and Negroes attend separate schools, the kind of secondary education provided for Negroes is intended to prepare them for opportunities·that are consistent with their caste status. One of the reasons why Booker T. Washington was able to do so much for Negro education was that he was willing to concede the white stipulation on this point.

This industrial education has not been without great value both to Negroes and to whites. The achievements of George Washington Carver alone, in revealing the resources of the humble peanut, have brought to the South economic returns that would pay a considerable fraction of the whole bill of Negro education.

In spite of the efforts that have been made by both public and private agencies to equalize educational opportunities for Negroes, the fact remains that the color line has not been erased and that its shadow is still over the schoolhouse. It is recognized

[2] *Democracy's Challenge to Education*, ed. by Beulah Amidon; "Crossroads Schools," by Farnsworth Crowder, p. 149.

that the race problem in the South is still a difficult and complicated one. But whatever the situation may be, the educational ideals of a democracy can never be fully realized in a society where a caste system is tolerated.

The third, and in many ways the most important factor that appears to determine the amount and kind of schooling that American youth receive, is the socio-economic status of their homes, the social class to which they belong. While it is true that America does not have a hereditary class system of aristocracy, as do England and other countries, and while social class distinctions are frowned upon, yet it is true that American homes and families can be divided into three or more class levels. These levels are determined in part by income, in part by family name and history, in part by positions of influence and prestige occupied by members of the family, and in part by the nature of the occupation of the father or family head. Recent studies of American communities have revealed definite social stratification of the population into as many as seven classes. It appears that as communities grow older and become more settled, class lines tend to become more fixed and class groups tend to remain more constant generation after generation. These social classes are measured off roughly but not accurately by instruments for determining socio-economic background, general culture, and occupational status. However, sociological research has not been carried far enough to reveal the extent to which American communities are socially stratified or the extent to which the stratification that does exist corresponds to the conventional measures of socio-economic background used in educational research. The facts reported below show the relation between socio-economic background and education and only indirectly reveal the relation of social class to education.

The facts are taken mainly from the American Youth Commission's Surveys in Maryland and Pennsylvania, and the Regents' Inquiry in the State of New York. The conclusions drawn cannot be generalized to other states unless it can be shown that comparable conditions exist. Before reporting the outcome of these surveys it may be noted that psychologists and sociologists have pretty well established the fact that in most American communities there is a considerable positive correlation between socio-economic status of homes and the intelligence of the children, their achievements in school, social attitude, and their character and personality development. In short, the most desirable outcomes of education seem best secured in children who come from the better homes—and on the contrary, maladjusted and problem children tend to come mainly from the underprivileged homes and sections of the community.

The evidence in support of this relationship between home background and school achievement, including character development and social adjustment, is well known and need not be summarized here. What seems to have been overlooked, however, is the apparent fact that children from the poor homes and lower class do not in fact have the same educational opportunities as children from the better homes. The facts collected by the surveys in the states of Maryland, Pennsylvania, and New York clearly show that not only do the children from the better homes spend more years in school but they are also enrolled in the curricula that lead to the higher occupations. These facts lead to the inescapable conclusion that the amount and kind of secondary education that many youth in these three states receive are determined to no small degree by the socioeconomic level of the homes from which they come. Before reporting the facts it may be said that the situation may not be the fault of the schools. It could be argued that the schools are free, the secondary curricula are elective, and attendance up to a certain age is compulsory. If the child from the poor home drops out early, or elects a course of study leading to a skilled trade rather than to a profession, that is his responsibility. On the other hand, if the child from the better home continues through high school and college and elects a curriculum leading to a profession, that is well and good, provided he can pass the work. The school, it may be said, has no responsibility for selecting and placing children in courses of study according to their talents.

But first let us look at the facts on which the above general conclusion is based. They may be conveniently summarized in the form of a series of propositions.

1. *The Regents' Inquiry in New York State showed that the five major curricula of the secondary schools form a distinct hierarchy and the children from the "better" homes are enrolled in higher curricula in greater proportions than in the*

lower curricula. And vice versa the children from the poorer homes tend to be concentrated in the lower curricula.

The most pertinent facts in support of this proposition are found in the volume, *High School and Life,* prepared for the Regents' Inquiry by Francis Spaulding of Harvard. Here are a few passages from Spaulding's excellent analysis of the secondary schools of New York State.

Analyses of the results of tests used by the Regents' Inquiry show that *at the time they leave school the graduates of the major curricula form a distinct academic hierarchy with the college preparatory graduates at the top and vocational, industrial, agricultural, and homemaking graduates at the bottom.*[3] . . . This academic hierarchy repeats itself in other matters than measurable school accomplishment. Ranked in terms of the socio-economic status of their homes, the college-preparatory pupils come highest in the scale and the vocational pupils lowest. Pupils enrolled in the academically "better" curricula are more likely to stay in school until they graduate than are pupils enrolled in curricula which are less select academically.[4]

In another volume of the Inquiry written by Ruth Eckert and Thomas O. Marshall we find the following:

Almost 85 percent of graduates in the college entrance curriculum, for example, came from homes judged to be 'moderate,' 'comfortable,' or 'wealthy,' one out of every three of the students ranking in the two upper categories. About one out of every seven general curriculum graduates lived in comfortable or wealthy homes, a proportion that decreases to one in twenty among those enrolled in other vocational curricula in general high schools. In even sharper contrast are the results for those pupils graduated from vocational schools. Fewer than one in thirty boys and none of the girls completing courses in these specialized schools were reported as coming from comfortable or wealthy homes. More than half of the boys and three-fourths of the girls who received vocational school diplomas were judged to be poor or indigent.[5]

The occupations of the parents of these pupils were rated on the Minnesota Occupational Scale which places them in a

[3] Francis T. Spaulding. *High School and Life;* publication of the Regents' Inquiry Into the Character and Cost of Public Education in the State of New York, 1938; p. 84.

[4] *Ibid.,* p. 86.

[5] Ruth E. Eckert and T. O. Marshall, *When Youth Leave School;* publication of the Regents' Inquiry, 1938, pp. 72-73.

hierarchy according to "social prestige values as well as by financial returns." This scale is an effort to rate homes by social status as well as by economic status. The highest value on the scale is + 2.23 and the lowest − 1.43. The mean of an unselected population is 0 and the standard deviation is 1.00.

When rated on this scale the pupils in the college preparatory curriculum averaged a score of + .80, those in the general curriculum + .50, those in the business and commercial curriculum + .07, and those in other vocational curricula + .03. These figures mean that there is a high correlation between the socio-economic status of the homes from which these children come and the secondary school curriculum in which they enroll. It is true that the class lines here are not sharply drawn, but in an unpublished study Lloyd Warner reports that, in a New England small city, there are no upper class children in the public high school at all, and that two-thirds of those from the upper middle class are enrolled in the Latin (i.e., college preparatory) curriculum; whereas only 11 percent of the lower class are enrolled in that curriculum. In the commercial curriculum are only 6 percent of the upper middle and 55 percent of the lower classes. In the face of these facts it is hard to believe that the various high school curricula select students on the basis of talent or capacities alone and that all students who have college brains get into the college curriculum, and that all who have the more mechanical talents of skilled laborers get into the vocational curriculum.

2. *The surveys in the states of Maryland, Pennsylvania, and New York show that there is a high positive correlation between the grade level at which youth drop out of school and the socio-economic level of their homes.*

The Maryland survey showed that two-thirds of the sons and daughters of the professional and upper class occupational groups completed college; while only fourteen percent of the sons and daughters of farm laborers completed the eighth grade. In fact, the correlation between the social and economic hierarchy of occupations and the percent of children who completed the eighth grade is nearly perfect. The same is true for the number who graduated from high school. The figures show that only sixteen out of twenty of the children of the upper occupational group graduated from high school; twelve out of twenty of the next occupational level; seven out of twenty of the next; and only two out of twenty of the lowest occupational group. The same story is repeated for college graduates. Of all the youth in the Maryland survey who went through college, 68.5 percent were sons and daughters of fathers whose occupations were in the professional or managerial group.

In the Pennsylvania survey a study of a sample of 8,978 youth who had dropped out of school before the second year of college showed a high positive correlation between the grade completed and the socio-economic status of their homes. Of those who completed the eighth grade 78 percent were from homes below average, while the corresponding figure for those who completed high school was 35 percent from homes below average. Of those who went through one year of college only 11 percent came from homes below average.

The data gathered by the Maryland and Pennsylvania surveys of the American Youth Commission on the relation between socio-economic status of homes and grades completed in schools are fully supported by the Regents' Inquiry. "So severely handicapped are withdrawing pupils that almost one out of every two belongs to a family classified as poor or indigent. Only one in twenty was reported to be living in comfortable or wealthy homes."[6]

"While encouraging variations occur occasionally, the great mass of adolescent boys and girls seem destined to maintain in their generation the economic hierarchy established for the preceding one."[7] There is a very high positive correlation between the mean scores on the Minnesota Occupational Status Scale and the grade level at which children dropped out of school.

"Any belief that the public secondary school is open on equal terms to all the children of all the people is seriously challenged by the steady increase, from grade to grade, in socio-economic status."[8]

3. *In Pennsylvania many youth from the better homes were continued in school beyond the time when they could profit by the kind of education the schools had to offer, and many from*

[6] Ruth E. Eckert and T. O. Marshall, *When Youth Leave School*, Regents' Inquiry, 1938, p. 72.
[7] *Ibid.*, p. 78.
[8] *Ibid.*, p. 84.

poorer homes dropped out before they had exhausted the benefits of the schools.

The Pennsylvania survey reported that out of every thousand youth studied who were of college age (and the sample was fairly representative) 154 were in college. Of these, 86 were qualified on the basis of intelligence tests, but 68 were of doubtful college ability. But for every 86 who were in college and of college ability, there were 174 who were qualified, but who had dropped out at the end of high school or before. The fact that intelligence test scores were available for a large percentage of the Pennsylvania youth studied enabled the investigators to estimate the double waste in education due on the one hand to failure to hold in school many youth of superior intelligence and, on the other hand, to the continuance in school of many who had inferior intelligence. One rather interesting bit of statistical evidence in this connection is the following: From one sample of 3,022 youth (all college age) on whom data were available as to grade completed, socio-economic status of homes measured by the Sims scale, and intelligence, I selected 555 who were above the average of that group in intelligence, but below the average on home background scores. Of this group 7.2 percent were in college. Then I selected all who were below average in intelligence and above average on the home background score (381) and found that 24.9 percent of this group were in college. The percentage of the whole group (3,022) who were in college was 20.84. While the sample is quite too small to be conclusive in itself, yet it confirms the general conclusion of the Pennsylvania Survey as to the double waste from continuing in school those who lack scholastic abilities, and allowing the dropping out of some of the more intellectually talented.

The surveys of the three states are in general agreement as to why youth drop out of school. There are many reasons, most of which are associated in one way or another with geographic location, race, and socio-economic background. Now the number of years a youth remains in school is a crude measure of the amount of his schooling. It is not a perfect measure, as we all know, but it is the best general measure available. Ideally a youth is quite justified in leaving school when he feels that it is no longer profitable for him to remain. For some youth the schools will have done about all they can in the way of developing talents by the end of the eighth grade, or certainly by the end of high school. It is no great loss in human resources if their schooling is terminated at that time. The great loss in human resources is incurred by those who for financial or other reasons are forced to drop out long before the values of schooling for them have been exhausted. This is shown roughly by the percentage of youth who had I.Q.'s of 100 or more at each level of leaving school. Of those who quit at the end of the

School grade completed	6	7	8	9	10	11	12	Fresh.
Per cent who had I.Q.'s of 100 or better	18	22	33	46	42	66	68	80

6th grade eighteen had I.Q.'s of 100 or more, etc. Of all who graduated from high school and did not go on to college 68 percent had I.Q.'s of 100 or higher.

Quoting from the author of the report on the Maryland survey,

Some of our most exciting success stories have been written about young men whose passion for getting on and whose capacity to absorb punishment have enabled them to "crash the gates" of the restrictions that have closed them in. The statesmanship of Lincoln and the poetry of Keats, arising from the humble depths of log cabins and stables, have not only been an inspiration to underprivileged youth, but they have led us to suspect that there must be some mysterious causal relationship between lowly beginnings and exalted goals. The facts suggest that the tendency is quite the reverse, and that the "gate crashers" are the rather lonely exceptions to the rule.[9]

With a little professional license, one might consider the factors that influence grade attainment as a miniature deck of cards. However this deck is shuffled, one card—one fact—will always be on top: the strongest single factor in determining how far a youth goes in school is the occupation of his father.

When the father's occupation is held constant, the differences between the grades attained by white and Negro youth are small compared with the differences in the grades attained by the youth with fathers in the various occupational groups. Moreover, the *range* between the median grades attained by youth of professional and farm laborer fathers is very much the same for all the groups considered—a difference of about five grades. Clearly it is

[9] Howard M. Bell, *Youth Tell Their Story.* Washington, D. C. American Council on Education, 1938, p. 96.

not primarily sex, race, nor place of residence, but rather the occupation of the father that accounts for these differences.[10]

4. Why youth say they leave school.

The Maryland surveyors asked 10,858 young people why they quit school. About half said they left for economic reasons; about one-fourth, because of lack of interest in school; and one-eighth, because they felt their education was complete. The author of the report is of the opinion that economic reasons are not quite as important as here indicated and is inclined to attach more weight to lack of school adjustment—indirectly such factors as lack of interest, feeling that nothing is being gained, disciplinary trouble, subjects too difficult, and the like. The reason for discounting the economic motive is the fact that only ten per cent of all youth interviewed said that they felt that their schooling was of no economic value, while thirty-two per cent said it was a great asset. There is, of course, a correlation between the economic value attached to school and grade reached, but the real reasons why youth leave school are to be found by digging deeper into family and social life and basic human motivations.

Let us glance once more at the essential facts: (1) the lower the home on the socio-economic scale the earlier the children drop out; (2) rural children, Negro children, and foreign-born urban children tend to drop out sooner than sons and daughters of native white; (3) those enrolled in the vocational and business curricula are less likely to graduate than those in the more "select" curricula; (4) the lower the pupil's scholastic accomplishment or aptitude the sooner he will drop out. This seemed to be true in New York but not in Pennsylvania, but the Pennsylvania survey showed that of those who dropped out at grades 6, 8, 11, 12, and freshman years respectively, the following percents made marks that were average or better: 40, 42, 46, 72, and 79; (5) the greater the number of undesirable personal traits and the fewer desirable traits of a pupil, the sooner he or she will drop out; (6) the less their teachers know about their home backgrounds and their out-of-school problems the sooner they drop out. In this connection one of the most significant findings of the Regents' Inquiry was the fact that

[10] Ibid., p. 63.

high schools know most about boys and girls from well-to-do homes,
who graduate from the college-preparatory curriculum; they know
least about young people from economically poor homes, who leave
school without graduating. The fullest information that the schols
gave about any single group of pupils was given about the boys
and girls who had spent an extra year in high school as post-
graduates in the college-preparatory curriculum. This is the group,
it will be recalled, which stands at the top of the academic hierarchy.
From this group down, the schools reported less and less completely
about each lower group in the hierarchy—general, fine arts, commercial, vocational. Furthermore, whatever the curricula which
the pupils had followed, the schools knew less about young people
whose homes stood low in the social scale than about those whose
homes stood high; less about pupils who had received school
marks below average than about those whose work had been better
than average.[11]

A series of "close-up" pictures of how social stratification
affects school life and work have been taken by Dollard and
Davis in a study of personality problems of Negro youth.[12]
These two investigators collected detailed life histories on
Negro adolescents which were supplemented by interviews
with parents, siblings, teachers, and friends. The purpose of the
study was to isolate the social, economic, and educational forces
that are molding the personalities of Negro youth. From previous sociological studies of Natchez, Mississippi, by Gardner and
Davis, and of Indianola, Mississippi, by Dollard it was shown
that there exists in southern cities, in addition to the caste
system which divides the whites from the Negroes, a class system
within each racial group. Among the Negroes there are at least
three distinct social classes—upper, middle, and lower—and
most Negroes are themselves well aware of the class to which
they belong. In *Children of Bondage*, which has just been published, there is a chapter on "Social Class and School-Learning"
which gives the close-up picture of why some children leave
school, why others continue, and why there are large differences in school achievements of children who have equal native
talents insofar as that can be determined.

[11] Francis T. Spaulding, *High School and Life.* Regents' Inquiry, 1938, pp.
159-60.
[12] John Dollard and Allison Davis, *Children and Bondage.* Publication of
the American Youth Commission. Washington, D. C. American Council on
Education, 1940.

The explanation suggested by these authors is quite simple. It is that children who are rewarded for remaining in school and anticipate punishments if they drop out, stay in school; and children who directly or indirectly are punished for going to school and rewarded for staying out, tend to drop out. These rewards and punishments are administered by three groups of people—parents, teachers, and friends or youth companions. The punishments are whipping and other forms of corporal attack, threats of all sorts, deprivations, withdrawal of love or support, disapproval, rebuke, nagging, and so on. The rewards are approvals, praise, caresses, positions of prestige like being assigned a part in a play or chosen to carry the flag, money rewards, and so on. They are the usual run of social rewards and punishments of daily life.

In studying Negro schools in New Orleans, Dollard and Davis found that low-class Negro children tend to drop out sooner than middle-class and upper-class children; that those enrolled in the more select curricula stay longer in school. In fact, each of the six factors found in the Regents' Inquiry and in the Maryland survey operate in these Negro schools. Close investigation reveals that the low-class Negro youth who were dropping out of school at the earliest opportunity did so because their school experiences were so bitter and distasteful to them. In short, they were receiving no rewards from teachers, parents, or friends; but on the contrary, punishments. The upper- and middle-class children, on the other hand, were being rewarded for school attendance and punished, especially by parents, for school failures. One reason being that to be a high school or college graduate is a distinct and definite middle- and upper-class symbol. It is one of the badges of class status and membership.

These studies seem to suggest that children who come from the better homes derive more satisfactions and reinforcements from school life than do children from the lower classes. They, therefore, enjoy school and tend to continue within. Those who do not enjoy it, but find it dull, irksome, and even painful, tend to avoid it and escape it as soon as they can.

Those who enjoy school are usually the ones who reward the teacher and from whom he derives satisfaction. Thus a circle of reinforcement is set up. The teacher rewards the pupil and the pupil rewards the teacher—or vice versa. Pupils from whose progress the teacher derives satisfactions are those he wants to know. Pupils from whose school progress the teacher derives no pleasure, those he does not want to know. Dollard and Davis point out that this "circular" reinforcement not only operates between teacher and pupils, but also between parent and child, and the playmate and child. They point out further that this circle of rewards is ordinarily confined within a class level. The teachers in the New Orleans schools for Negroes were mostly middle-class girls. This fact is important for teacher-pupil relations.

Dollard and Davis tell us that:

The Negro lower-class child is usually not allowed by his teacher to make the goal responses of privilege. He sees the upper-class and upper-middle-class children being accorded preference, not only in classroom recitations but also in school entertainments and in intimate friendship relations with the teacher. He finds that he is not granted these privileges; instead, he is stigmatized by teachers and their favored students on grounds of the "ignorance" of his parents, the dialect which he speaks, the appearance of his clothes, and, very likely, the darkness of his skin. It does not take him long to discover that something is wrong and that the teacher's "pets" of high status are the only ones who can make the prestige goal responses. If there is no reward for learning, in terms of privilege and anxiety-reduction, there is no motive for work. The lower-class child soon becomes a "dummy." Frequently he is openly aggressive toward the teacher; if not, he plays hooky, and he displaces his aggression from the powerful teacher to the more vulnerable upper-class and upper-middle-class pupils. He becomes like his parents, "bad" and "ignorant."

When he reaches adolescence, moreover, the lower-class child is no longer subjected to punishment by his parents to make him study, and his anxiety concerning school learning is virtually extinguished. The child knows also that his parents cannot afford to support him after eight or ten years of schooling. He has learned that his parents' friends, their minister, their club officers, and they themselves are only semiliterate; as a result, his own ceiling of educational aspiration is low. The child usually identifies with these symbolic adults; his anxiety is therefore extinguished *when he has attained or just surpassed their educational status*.[13]

The report of the Regents' Inquiry calls attention to the

[13] John Dollard and Allison Davis, *Children of Bondage*. Washington, D. C., publication of the American Youth Commission, 1940, pp. 283, 285.

well-known fact that American secondary schools were built from the top down. They were first primarily college preparatory schools, and their curricula were organized to fit the entrance requirements of liberal arts colleges. But the pattern of liberal arts education in American colleges was borrowed from the European universities—notably Oxford and Cambridge in England. Here university education was designed for those who were "free" from the necessity of having to work for a living, that is, the aristocratic leisure class. The English system of higher education, especially during the eighteenth and nineteenth centuries, was aristocratic. It was not intended for the common people. But we borrowed it for our American colleges and then proceeded to cut the pattern of secondary education to fit it. This accounts in no small degree for the fact that the college preparatory course in the New York State high school is even today regarded as the "élite" course of study.

In some states, however, the secondary schools are gradually acquiring independence of the liberal arts colleges and are offering to youth of their respective communities a wider range of educational electives. The trend in secondary education is toward a wider service to youth and therefore toward the democratic ideal. But much remains to be done. Not only should the school offer courses for the youth who lack the college preparatory talents but have others, but it must also make the so-called non-academic curricula more respectable.

The democratic ideal in education, therefore, cannot be reached until each American youth, regardless of where he lives, the race to which he belongs or the home from which he comes, is offered an opportunity both to develop his talents with dignity and respect and to find an occupation in which he can serve society best and with greatest satisfaction to himself. This second phase of the democratic process—that of finding a job according to one's education—must await another occasion for discussion.

Program for the Attainment of American Educational Ideals

By

WILLIAM G. CARR, Ph.D.*

EVERYONE seems to agree that concerted efforts should be directed promptly and with the greatest possible vigor to strengthening loyalty to democracy among all of the citizens of the United States; that if we lack an intelligent and active loyalty, then a two-ocean navy and a million men under arms will be of little value indeed; and that the principal means which we have available for developing this all-important loyalty is our system of public schools and colleges.

The provision of an adequate program of citizenship education for every American boy and girl and for every adult, as he may need such education, is the American ideal. Our schools thus provide not only the finest example of democracy in action, but also its most certain and invulnerable defense. The question which I have been asked to discuss, however, is one of ways and means rather than the general question of the advisability of an effective program of education. In theory, we have already signed on the dotted line our endorsement of education and its great purposes of citizenship and human development. Practice, however, falls short of that ideal. The best schools come as close perhaps as human institutions can; the worst schools miss the bus entirely. How can we shorten the gap between our ideals of good education for American democracy and our actual practice? Here is an intensely practical problem, the complete solution of which will call for all the idealism of the American people and for all the skill and leadership that the teaching profession can muster.

It would be possible to discuss this practical question from a variety of aspects. One might consider, for example, the undoubted weaknesses in the administrative structure of our edu-

* Secretary, Educational Policies Commission, Washington, D. C.

cational system and the means whereby these weaknesses can be removed. Or one might probe the defects in the relation of our public school system to government agencies and to public opinion, and suggest ways in which these barriers might be overcome. Again, we might talk about the financing of education, which is in a most unstable, inadequate, and inequitable condition in many of the states of the Union, and we might draw upon the studies of experts in public finance and taxation to devise a remedy for this particular area of weakness. In the limited time available, however, I wish to offer for your consideration some observations regarding the improvement of the educational program itself rather than the improvement of the administrative and financial aspects of the question.

The Educational Policies Commission during the past five years has centered its work on the relationship of education to various aspects of American democracy.

Within the framework of its four basic publications, the Commission has developed a program for the improvement of civic education. This program began to take shape a year ago when a staff of six persons began a series of field studies covering the work of ninety selected secondary schools located in twenty-seven states. The report of this study, *Learning the Ways of Democracy*, will be published this month. The Commission will follow up this report with a series of about thirty regional conferences to carry to teachers, school officials, and the general public in every part of the country an informed enthusiasm for the teaching of effective citizenship.

It is helpful to identify fairly clearly five aspects of the citizenship education program as it exists in a typical American high school. First, we have those methods of teaching in the classroom which may be in themselves experiences in democratic living. Second, we must consider those activities which occur in the school, but outside of regular classes, including student government and a wide range of extracurricular activities which may contribute to citizenship education. In the third place, we have the participation of school youth in community activities outside of the school building, but under the general auspices of the school or, at least, with its encouragement. Fourth, we have the methods used for testing or evaluating the outcomes of citizenship education, methods which are often highly influential in determining processes and goals. Finally, there is the content of the course of study—that is to say, what is actually taught about citizenship and about democracy in courses in the social studies or in other subjects.

1. TEACHING METHODS

Teaching facts and theories about democracy will be of little effect if the environment in which pupils live in the classroom negates those ideals which are taught by textbook or by preachment. The ideal of democracy in the State, in order to be an impelling motive for the individual, must be grounded in a multitude of actual experiences in democratic living in smaller face-to-face groups.

How can democratic teaching be identified and encouraged?

In the first place, democratic teaching involves coöperative action for the common good. Democracy can become more effective when we learn to coöperate better. Many methods of teaching, steeped in tradition, stress competition. Marks of distinction are showered on the pupil who surpasses his fellows. Our schools usually give prizes to the one who wins the most credit for himself, rarely to the one who can work most effectively with others. We pin the badge of failure on the child who is defeated in competition rather than on the child who fails to learn how to coöperate.

Of course, there is a place for competition as a motivating force in education. People need a reasonable amount of self-assurance and self-reliance. The immediate need in many schools is for a better balance between coöperation and competition. Children should learn through experience as directly as possible and at an early stage of their lives that the combined efforts of a coöperating group can often solve problems that the ablest individual in the group cannot possibly handle unaided.

Another hallmark of democratic teaching is mutual friendliness and respect as shown by students to one another and as revealed in the relations between students and teachers. Democratic teaching requires teachers who think deeply and care sincerely about the democratic ideal and its implications for life in America today. It requires teachers who are willing to submit their own familiar teaching practices to unsparing scrutiny in the light of this ideal. It requires, above all, teachers who will boldly reject the fiction of mass education, who know full well that while there may be mass instruction, democratic education works for the individual and with the individual. Parenthetically, the school organization and the teaching load should be so adjusted that teachers may become acquainted with their students and develop friendly and human relations with them.

A third characteristic of democratic teaching is that all members of the group share according to their respective abilities and maturities in planning, executing, and evaluating the results. Children are not born with the skills of democratic living; they must learn them. Biological heredity seems to provide no mechanism for transmitting social ideals and institutions. We do not inherit democracy in the way that we may inherit blue eyes or curly hair. We learn this difficult way of life in only one way—by thoughtful practice under competent guidance. It would, of course, be unwise to expect first-grade children to take complete responsibility for planning and carrying out their work. But it is an even greater folly to impose all plans, courses, and methods on all students because "they are too immature to know what is best for them." The goal to which growth should be directed is a matured civic responsibility by the end of high school. This will never be accomplished as long as we keep our children in leading strings, as long as we tell them every day what they are to do, how they are to do it, and when they are to do it, without giving them a chance to ask why or to share in the direction of their own education. Practice—purposeful guided practice—makes perfect, in learning citizenship as in other learnings.

A fourth characteristic of democratic teaching is its use of the experimental method of free inquiry, resting on a faith in informed intelligence. It will be necessary, if we are to examine all sides of various controversial questions, to have much better school libraries and to use them much more widely. It will require a wider range of reference works and a greater variety of viewpoints. In the study of controversial matters the radio should become a potent teaching aid and more use should be made of newspapers, news magazines, magazines which give large space to public questions, and various series of pamphlets on public issues.

The democratic classroom is ventilated by the winds of freedom. We aspire to a society in which public policy is ultimately determined by the enlightened will of the people. To deny to any portion of the people the right to discuss and consider controversial questions or to place any public question outside the pale of free discussion, is to strike a death blow at the heart of our institutions. The very nature of controversy implies that there are differences of opinion. At the points of greatest controversy, the decisions of greatest importance are made. To exclude the people from free discussion of controversial issues is, therefore, to deny them the right of thinking on problems at the very points where such thought is most important. If the people have not this right, they are unable to make intelligent decisions. The free election becomes a controlled plebiscite, and power passes into the hands of individuals who are adroit enough and unscrupulous enough to take it and use it. American high schools and the public which supports them must recognize the crucial importance of giving young people an opportunity to learn through practice to deal in a democratic way with debatable issues, to think clearly and honestly and fairly and unselfishly about these issues, to gather information which bears on them, and to reach decisions. Have we enough faith in our institutions to believe that they can stand critical examination and that where these institutions are working badly they can be improved within the framework of the democratic process?

We hear a good deal of jittery talk these days about subversive activities and subversive agencies. Some ill-informed people have even hinted that the schools are subversive.

What is subversive? If we recall our Latin derivatives, we see that this adjective applies to the process of "overturning from the foundation." What is the foundation of the future of our democracy? Does it not rest, finally and completely, on educated citizens? I conclude, therefore, that a minority which might, for selfish reasons, attack or weaken the public schools would be attacking the foundations of democracy. And they who dare to do that, knowingly or unknowingly, are the real subversive agents, in whatever disguise they may appear. Yes, though they carry banners inscribed with the magic word "economy"; though with patriotic gestures they wrap themselves in the folds of the flag itself; though they burn incense before the most conspicuous altars of liberty: still they remain under every disguise the enemies of that evolving democracy which we wish to insure for ourselves and our posterity. I do not for a moment suggest that it is unpatriotic to criticize the schools with a view to their improvement. I do suggest that those who assume this responsibility are morally obligated to acquaint themselves with the facts in the situation and to avoid with great care irresponsible and untruthful assertions which would undermine and eventually destroy the educational foundations of democracy itself.

So far in our discussion of a democratic classroom we have placed our emphasis on freedom and rights. There is another equally important aspect—responsibility. In the democratic classroom, responsibility in action is coupled with freedom in thought. There is a small high school in the Pacific Northwest where every Monday is a free work day and practically no formal classes are held. The students determine for themselves what they should do during the school hours, what they will work at, and which teachers they will consult for guidance and assistance. Everyone saves for these days the many small jobs not completed during the preceding week. There is no disorder. Little time is wasted. In another high school there is organized a "self-reliance group" which provides another example of responsible action coupled with freedom. Any student may apply in writing for admission to this group. The home-room of this student votes on whether the applicant qualifies. The home-room teacher and the principal of the school also pass on the application. After these three approvals are given the student becomes a member of the group. He then has full responsibility for managing his own affairs. Class attendance is optional. He may leave the school grounds whenever he thinks he should. The members of this group have shown their ability to direct their own activities in the school, and they are therefore entitled to freedom commensurate with this willingness to assume responsibility. The privilege of being a self-reliant student is highly coveted, and in several years of operation the plan has developed worthwhile characteristics of citizenship in the children of that high school.

2. EXTRACURRICULAR ACTIVITIES

Few people need to be convinced that extracurricular activities may be of tremendous importance in achieving educational values. However, in relatively few schools do these activities actually deliver all the values that they might. Student organizations may be found in the schools of all countries of the world—those which accept democracy, and those which reject it. It follows that student organizations in themselves do not guarantee good education for American citizens. Like any other part of the educative process such activities must be directed to some purpose.

The ultimate responsibility of the professional staff for the conduct of student activities in a secondary school cannot be evaded. For example, if candidates for a student office conduct a campaign which reflects the cheap and harmful methods of some adult politicians, that activity should be discouraged and, if serious and necessary, even restrained. There is no more excuse for allowing students to practice bad government in their student organizations than there is to allow them to practice bad grammar in their English class or inaccurate addition in a mathematics class.

This viewpoint, of course, does not by any means exclude the possibility of helping students to learn by making their own mistakes and by suffering the necessary consequences of their errors. But there is a vast difference between deliberate teaching of this kind and the abdication of professional responsibility on the specious plea that student activities are undemocratic if the faculty takes any interest in them.

This recommendation may be elaborated to apply to various special cases. For example, unusual care is necessary in connection with student courts and student discipline. Such activities can easily give practice in undesirable and undemocratic procedures. The enforcement of law and the administration of justice are necessary civic activities which youth should study, if possible, through actual practice. Yet a student court which is more concerned with penalties than with prevention, or which acts in an arbitrary or prejudiced fashion is not providing good education either for the members of the court or for the offenders. If schools are to have student courts and police at all, skilled and watchful adult guidance should be provided in order that such activities may give practice in the highest possible type of civic behavior.

3. SCHOOL YOUTH AND THE LIFE OF THE COMMUNITY

Every experienced high school teacher or principal knows, as he watches students come and go, that one of the great problems of our schools is the deterioration which often occurs when graduates enter adult life. Why is it, we ask, that many students who are leaders in student citizenship have so little interest in civic affairs after they graduate? Why is it that their ideals of democracy become so quickly tarnished and forgotten? One explanation for this loss in effectiveness is the extreme insularity of the school. Many schools are pedagogical islands cut off by deep channels of convention from the world which surrounds them. The drawbridge is lowered only at specified hours. The inhabitants of these islands rarely venture to cross the guarded moat during school hours. To be sure, they read about the surrounding world in books and they return to live on the mainland when school is out, but few schools have built bridges over which two-way traffic may freely pass between school and community. There is no denying, of course, that the school must provide a controlled environment, different from that in the world at large, in order that students may gain rapidly the maximum of the necessary learning and growth while they are in the school. There is no justification for a school which is just as bad as the community which surrounds it or where students do only the things which they would do if they were not in school. But if this necessary control of the environment results in isolation from the real social and economic problems of the community, it defeats its own purpose.

Furthermore, few schools attempt to follow their students after the graduation exercises. If the graduate goes on to college, the responsibility for his further guidance is passed on to the higher institution. If he goes to work or enters the army of the unemployed, he is often left to find his way alone in a puzzling network of economic and political institutions which, he may vaguely remember, he once read something about in a school textbook. There *is* a gap between the school and the outside world. Can it be bridged, even better, can it be filled in so that the separation between the school and the community will disappear?

Schools *can* span the gap which isolates their teaching from the life of the communities about them. But the bridge must be solidly built. The community activities of youth should confront them with real and challenging problems, problems which directly affect the student's own welfare and that of his family, or problems which concern him as a member of the community. These problems should not be artificial exercises. The students must be convinced that what they do will make a difference—an important and wholesome difference in somebody's life. An effective program of school and community activity requires that the participants be able to do something about the problems they face. To be sure, they may not be able to solve them completely, but they can at least take a first step toward a solution or perform their own part in carrying through an action that requires the coöperation of many people.

School programs of community activity should go beyond the immediate problem and seek to define and grapple with deeper issues. This is especially important when the activities consist of help of some sort to the unfortunate. It is splendid that high school students should make collections of food and money to give to those less fortunate than themselves, but the alleviation of this suffering is best accompanied by a study of the causes which bring about poverty, ill health, ignorance, and unemployment. Lacking such study, school charitable activities may become a degrading routine to both givers and recipients.

4. EVALUATION OF RESULTS

High standards of individual achievement and the rigorous evaluation of results are by no means repugnant to a democracy. If a student fails to show a growth in civic education and behavior which is proportionate to his ability, disapproval, tempered though it may be by understanding guidance, may be expected from his companions and his teachers who are genuinely concerned about his welfare and the welfare of society. The purpose of such an evaluation should be understood by all who are party to it—students, teachers, parents, and research specialists. Whenever possible and appropriate, those who are evaluated should share in developing the means and the processes of evaluation. This in itself may be an educational experience of great value.

As far as possible the evaluation of results in civic education, as in any other field of education, should be thoroughly impartial. All types of valid and reliable objective instruments should be employed whenever they are available. However, we should not depend exclusively on such instruments. Our objectives should not be determined by the availability of tests. When we are confronted with a choice between an objective testing machine which is remotely, if at all, related to the basic purposes of citizenship education, and bold reliance on the best judgment of observers who are thoroughly familiar with the purposes of civic education, we should unhesitatingly choose the latter. We should never fall into the error of the teacher who said, "I admit that it is desirable to teach good citizenship, but I don't see how I can teach it because I do not know how to test it." We should recognize, once and for all, that the standardized testing instruments are servants of the educational process and not its masters.

5. THE COURSE OF STUDY

It was not a function of our investigation to make a detailed survey of the social studies curriculum or to analyze and tabulate the many varieties of course of study material which might in some way contribute to better living for the individual citizen or toward the solution of social problems. We were concerned, however, with discovering what the schools are teaching about democracy itself. We wanted to know, for example, whether civics classes were teaching about the Bill of Rights and if so, what they were teaching. We tried to find out what direct instruction about democratic ideals, if any, was being given in the schools. We asked whether the schools were studying how well democracy works. We were eager to learn whether the relation of democracy to our modern technological society and its economic dislocations was also within the purview of the interests of the schools. We attempted to ascertain where, if at all, these topics were dealt with in their course of study, the kinds of materials that were presented to the students, and the degree to which these educational experiences were general or limited to a selected group of pupils. In the pursuit of such material we have gone through many thousand pages of courses of study from the schools involved and the citizenship education report will include illustrative excerpts from some of the best material of this nature that we have been able to find.

America's Town Meeting of the Air recently conducted a contest in which 6,000 high school students submitted essays on "What Is Democracy?" That so large a number of students attempted to answer the question and that the winning essays were of high quality are encouraging. But beyond this 6,000 there is a vast body of other young people. In order to discover what some of these run-of-the-mine students are thinking, we asked 2,000 high school students in 68 different classes in 40 schools, to write brief statements of what democracy means to them. The pupils were selected at random. They were given ample time to write brief answers. Their replies were anonymous so that they might be frank and papers were collected on the spot to avoid possibility of coaching or consultation.

The classification of responses provides opportunity for thought. Nine out of every ten students had some reasonably clear ideas about democracy and were able to express them on short notice. Only one reply in ten consisted of quotations of memorized statements, hopelessly confused wording, statements which were too vague for classification or failure to answer. These results are encouraging.

However, of the 90 percent that gave intelligible definitions, over two-thirds defined democracy solely in terms of political rights and liberties. Fewer than one-third gave evidence of an awareness that in a democracy citizens have obligations as well as rights. This condition requires immediate correction. Personal liberties will not long endure without widespread assumption of civic responsibility.

One is impressed also by the fact that practically all of the students who defined democracy seemed to be aware chiefly of its moral and political implications, most of them making reference to political institutions such as universal suffrage and consent of the governed. However, only 8 percent of the total said anything relating to the economic foundations of democracy, and of these, 3 out of 4 wrote of economic privilege, and only one out of 4 of economic responsibility.

Here are two inspiring examples of these youngsters' papers:

What does democracy mean to me? This morning, after eating my breakfast, I went out on the porch and picked up our newspaper. I read not what I was told to read, but news given freely with many opinions. I then came to school. I went into a large library without showing any kind of passes or permits. I used one of many excellent books on history. On my way to my homeroom I met and talked to several of my fellow students who may be richer or poorer than I. They may have a different religious belief or may have no religious belief at all. From my homeroom period I went to my history class. There I and the entire class discussed freely our subject of study for the entire period. That's what democracy means to me.

Democracy means allowing all persons an equal opportunity for political activity; a share in the government of their country; an equal opportunity to earn a living and to accumulate wealth; an equal opportunity to enjoy good health and recreation. It gives the individual the right to lead his life, to worship his God, in the way that he chooses without asking permission from any man. In return for the privileges that he gets, he shoulders an equal load of responsibilities. He must take an active part in the government, either as a voter or as an elected or appointed officer; he must see to it that what he does in leading his life in his own way does not act so as to do harm to others. In having an equal opportunity himself, he likewise has the responsibility of seeing that others enjoy the same privileges, to protect those privileges and to aid his nation to preserve itself.

Answers such as the foregoing are most encouraging. How many adults could, within 15 minutes or so, write definitions of democracy in any way comparable to those of these junior and senior high school youngsters?

I would like to close with another answer which is not such an excellent definition of democracy, but which contains, I hope, both unconscious humor and a reliable forecast for the future. A student in the Middle West wrote the following in response to our request for a definition of democracy: "Democracy means *liberty*, *equality*, and *eternity*, and I think our country has lived up to all three."

The schools of America have, in the past, done a great deal to achieve the liberty and equality of which this young high school student wrote. What is being done now and what is done in the next year or two in these same schools, will have much to do with determining whether the young man's identification of our democracy with eternity was sound prophecy.

If the spirit of democracy can elevate and refine the daily life of the classroom so that it not only teaches, but *is* democracy, with an unshakable faith in the worth and value of each child and adult that it touches; if we can provide students with actual practice in good government in the management of their own affairs; if we can keep the school and the community near enough together so that the two educational institutions may avoid working at cross purposes and may supplement each other's efforts; if we can be so clear of our ultimate objectives that measurement and testing will become a tool rather than an end; and if we can teach the truth about the accomplishments, the values, and the needs of our democracy, we shall be on our way to accomplishing the broad outlines of a program for the attainment of American educational ideals.

Pennsylvania and Switzerland: The American Origins of the Swiss Constitution

By

WILLIAM E. RAPPARD, LL.D.*

THE debt of constitutional gratitude which Switzerland owes the United States in general and Philadelphia in particular is such that it can never be repaid. Is it not fitting, however, that it should at least be recalled by a Swiss student of political science, when honored by an invitation to present a paper on the occasion of the bicentennial exercises of the University of Pennsylvania?[1]

The subject is essentially historical, as all political science necessarily must be if it wishes to be, to remain or perhaps—shall I say?—to become worthy of its name. But the subject is far from dead. It is alive not only in the grateful memory of the Swiss people everywhere. It is most alive also in that it deals with a problem of federalism. Are not problems of international federalism less dead than ever in this year of world tragedy?

INTRODUCTION

In 1848 the Swiss ship of state, after a stormy voyage of over five hundred and fifty years, at last came to port. It found refuge in the constitutional harbor which had been discovered and charted by the American statesmen assembled in the Continental Congress in Philadelphia more than half a century before. The story of this memorable docking, which took exactly fifty years, is not unknown. In fact all school children

* Professor of Public Finance, University of Geneva; Director of the Postgraduate School for International Studies, Geneva.

[1] The author is deeply grateful to his friend and colleague Professor E. M. Patterson for his great kindness in seeing these pages through the press.

in Switzerland are taught the lesson of how the loose con-
federacy of sovereign cantons, which had emerged from the
Middle Ages, survived throughout the religious wars of the
sixteenth and seventeenth centuries, momentarily succumbed
to the onslaughts of the French Revolution at the end of
the eighteenth, and was finally transformed in 1848 into
the federal state it is today. Nor are they ignorant of the fact
that this transformation was carried out in conscious and deliberate imitation of the American model.

My purpose in this paper is not to sum up the constitutional
history of Switzerland from 1798, when she first ceased to be
a confederation of sovereign cantons, until 1848. To do so
would merely be to repeat what is to be found in countless
textbooks and to add nothing to the knowledge of the subject.
Rather would I recall the most significant references to the
American precedent made in public discussion in Switzerland
in the course of that half-century and to show how and why it
finally prevailed.

Even in this field so strictly limited, I raise no claim to
complete originality. The influence of the United States on
the constitutional development of Switzerland is not only obvious in the light of contemporary testimony, as we shall see
presently. It has also struck many subsequent commentators
and through their writings it has become incorporated in the
common stock of historical information.[2] What has never been
attempted before, however, neither in English nor in any of
the national languages of Switzerland, is an inquiry devoted
exclusively to what might be called the case of American-Swiss

[2] The first and most important work on the constitutional similarities between the United States and Switzerland was that published in three volumes
by Professor J. J. Rüttimann under the title *Das nordamerikanische Bundes-
staatsrecht verglichen mit den politischen Einrichtungen der Schweiz* (Zurich,
1867, 1872, 1876). This monumental work is particularly significant in that its
author, thoroughly conversant with the American literature of his time, had,
before his academic career in Zurich, been active and prominent in Swiss
politics. As a member of the Zurich executive, he had attended the federal
Diet which drafted the constitution of 1848. A more recent and briefer study
is that of Professor Ed. His, *Amerikanische Einflüsse im Schweizerischen Ver-
fassungsrecht* (Basle, 1920). Cf. also my studies *Notre grande république soeur*,
(Geneva, 1916); *Suisse et Etats-Unis* (Geneva, 1916), *On some economic and
political relations between Switzerland and the United States* (New York, 1917);
*Le contrôle de la constitutionnalité des lois fédérales par le juge aux Etats-Unis
et en Suisse* (Basle, 1934). The latest book on the subject is an excellent doctor's
dissertation prepared in Zurich by an American exchange student, M. L. Tripp,
The Swiss and United States federal constitutional systems (Paris, 1940).

constitutional contagion of 1798-1848. What my study thus loses in scope it may, I hope, regain in novelty, thoroughness and convincing clarity.

THE REVOLUTIONARY PERIOD, 1798-1803

In the early months of 1798, Switzerland, which for over five centuries had been a league of sovereign cantons more even than a confederation,[3] was violently converted into a unitary state. That conversion was due to the will of a foreign conqueror. Revolutionary France, in imposing upon Switzerland the constitution of the "one and indivisible Helvetic Republic," was actuated by motives exclusively French. It was not in the slightest the will to adapt the new constitution to the needs and preferences of the Swiss governments nor even of the "emancipated" Swiss people that dictated its terms. It was the desire to imitate the French model of the year III, to suppress the influence of the former cantonal governments, which were both attached to their local sovereignties and hostile to the French Revolution, and to unify in order the more readily to rule from without. These motives alone explain the establishment in Switzerland of an highly centralized state on the ruins of all her traditional institutions.

Although completely foreign in origin, the constitution of 1798 none the less produced far-reaching and lasting but somewhat contradictory consequences. On the one hand the principles of liberty and equality which it implanted soon struck roots among a people well prepared by their historical antecedents to appreciate them. But, on the other hand, on account both of its foreign origin and of its foreign tendencies, the document as a whole was profoundly distasteful to the nation. As a result, not only the centralization and the uniformity but also the bicameral system which it introduced were for generations associated in the public mind with invasion, humiliation and everything that was loathsome. Thus it tended to confirm the Swiss people in their fidelity to their political traditions. Of these, cantonal sovereignty and unicameral legislation were perhaps the most firmly established.

[3] Lord Bryce recalls that in the Pennsylvania Convention of 1788, James Wilson had rejected the Swiss precedent by declaring truly that "the Swiss cantons are connected only by alliances." James Bryce, *The American Commonwealth* (3rd ed.; New York, 1905), vol. I, p. 23.

If any proof were needed of the general unpopularity of the constitution of 1798, it would be found in its frailty. As soon as, and indeed even before French military support failed it, it proved unworkable. The result was a period of chaos which lasted until 1803.

During this brief period, while six successive constitutions[4] were drafted, discussed and adopted, the circumstances were such that none was ever truly tried out. The country, which was on several occasions a European battlefield, was always occupied by foreign troops and its people, therefore, were never fully their own masters.

Constitutional debates, however, were constantly raging, not only in the federal legislature, but also in the form of journalistic and pamphletary controversy. In spite of the wild, passionate and often irresponsible character of these discussions, it is not impossible to note their general trend.

From this time on until the adoption of the Constitution of 1848 and indeed until the present day, the Swiss people have always been divided on the issue of greater or lesser political and administrative centralization. In the first years of the nineteenth century, these two opposing views were represented by parties called "Unitarians" and "Federalists."[5] The former favored the maintenance of the unitary state as set up in 1798; the latter the reassertion of cantonal sovereignty and the return to conditions more or less similar to those prevailing before the French revolutionary intervention.

Of these two parties, the former was by far the less numerous. It consisted mainly of individual intellectuals who had hailed with joy the French Revolution of 1789 and who hoped and trusted that it would, in Switzerland as elsewhere, bring about an era of enlightened freedom and rational justice. Most of them belonged to a class of university graduates who, under the traditional aristocratic institutions, had by reason of their birth been debarred from political activity. As long as they were assured of French support, this group governed the country.

[4] They are reprinted in Carl Hilty, *Oeffentliche Vorlesungen über die Helvetik* (Berne, 1878), pp. 729-787.

[5] Thus the Swiss Unitarians were the equivalent of the American Federalists and the Swiss Federalists that of the American Anti-Federalists! The difference of political outlook in the two countries is curiously reflected in this contradictory phraseology.

For a short time they were the main representatives of those regions which the constitution of 1798 had raised from the status of subject provinces to the dignity of new and equal cantons. At first they even seemed to be the national spokesmen of the major part of the peasantry everywhere, who were to be relieved of the burden of tithes and other traditional land charges. It soon became apparent, however, that there was no real solidarity between the ignorant masses of the country folk, bent almost exclusively on the improvement of their material lot, and their unchosen urban leaders who, voicing the wishes of the upper middle classes, were liberals indeed but not in the least democrats. It soon became apparent also that the only convinced Unitarians were these liberals. Conscious both of their intellectual superiority and of their numerical weakness, they were in favor of a form of government in which they hoped that the former would count for more and the latter for less.

As one of the most distinguished of them, Albrecht Rengger, a former Minister of the Interior, wrote to another highly cultured leader of the party, Philip Stapfer, minister in Paris, on December 19, 1802:

The class of men of culture, who demand a liberal order of things and who are capable of running it, is so limited that, distributed in the various cantons, they could not hold their own against the friends of privilege and the rabid patriots; they can achieve something only if united in one field of action.[6]

This party remained in control only as long as the French favored the unitary form of government in Switzerland. When, after the 18th of Brumaire, Bonaparte, dropping his revolutionary mask, more and more openly adopted reactionary policies at home, he also more and more clearly favored the Federalists in Switzerland at the expense of the liberal Unitarians, derided as ideological metaphysicians.

The Federalist party was led by the class which, for centuries, had ruled the sovereign cantons. Moreover, the masses, for a time allured by the prospects of liberty and equality held out to them by the French Revolution, were still Federalists at heart. They were so by national tradition, by habit and by

[6] *Leben und Briefwechsel von Albrecht Rengger,* ed. by Ferdinand Wyler (Zurich, 1847), vol. II, p. 82.

local prejudice. It is therefore not surprising to find Frédéric César Laharpe, one of the most influential Unitarians, appealing, on March 9, 1798, to the French General commanding the invading forces to replace "the gothic helvetic confederation, mother of all evils, by an indivisible republic uniting all the peoples of Switzerland" and adding: "Ah! citizen General, protect us against the double curse of the federalist oligarchy and of a frenzied demagogy."[7]

In the heat of this controversy, the recently adopted American federal system, which was coming to be known, was expressly repudiated by the thoroughgoing Unitarians and deliberately ignored by the thoroughgoing conservative Federalists. The latter would of course have nothing to do with a complicated newfangled foreign scheme of revolutionary origin, which was contrary to all Swiss traditions. But the rationalist Unitarians, for whom neither its novelty nor its complexity nor its foreign revolutionary origin were in themselves objections, were opposed to it because, if adapted to Swiss conditions it would tend to transfer back too much power to the cantons and thus dangerously promote political reaction.

Of these rabid Unitarians, one of the most outspoken and one of the most interesting for our purposes was Jean-Jacques Cart, a native of Morges, a little town situated on the banks of the Lake of Geneva, in the newly founded canton of Vaud. Cart, after studying law in Geneva, had become tutor of the son of the British General Wood, whom he accompanied to America. After spending four years in Boston from 1769 to 1773, he returned home to practice law in his native town. Here he published a pamphlet in which he challenged the right of the Bernese authorities to tax their Vaudois subjects without the consent of the latter. Obliged to flee to France, in 1791, in order to avoid arrest, he became acquainted with several of the Girondin leaders there. In 1793, Monge, who was then Minister of the Navy, entrusted him with a mission to the United States for the purchase of supplies for the French Government. Having lost his job when the Girondin Monge was replaced by his more extreme opponents, Cart settled down as a farmer in New York State.[8] He tells us himself

---

[7] J. Strickler, *Aktensammlung aus der Zeit der helvetischen Republik* (Berne, 1886), vol. I, p. 449.

[8] *Lettres de J. J. Cart à F. C. Laharpe* (Lausanne, 1799), p. 9.

how the revolution of 1798 brought him back to Switzerland. In a little book published in 1802 he wrote:

In June 1798 I left my woods and my plough in Ulster County; in twenty-eight days I was in Bordeaux and soon in Aarau [then the Swiss capital]. One afternoon, I called on citizen director Ochs. He received me in bed, I don't know why, since he was in perfect health. We spoke of Washington, of Hancock, of Adams, of Jefferson and of the Americanized Genevese Gallatin, truly worthy of his fate![9]

In October 1799, Cart became a member of the Swiss Senate. He took a very active part in its debates and constantly drew on his American experience in his speeches. Although full of admiration for everything American and especially for the republican simplicity which he had found abroad and which he sadly missed among his political associates on his return home, he was opposed to the idea of Switzerland's copying the American constitution. He wrote:

In America one hardly notices the existence of government. It has no agents anywhere, justices of the peace see to the arrest and imprisonment of anyone who troubles the public peace, which is rarely troubled. The highroads are safer than anywhere else, theft is rare, murder almost unknown.

Since 1800 there exists a capital of the general confederation, the federal capital of Washington. None of the republics which constitute it has a real capital. That would offend against the principle of equality.

During the five years I spent in the republic of New York, the seat of its government was successively established in New York City, in Albany and in Poughkeepsie.

One of my friends was secretary of the Senate. Once a year he would set off from his home in my surroundings. His travelling bag contained the archives and the records of the Senate. Three months later he was back home . . .

No pomp, no external show. Washington, president of the Congress, was dressed as Washington presiding over his plough; no body-guard, no drums, no noise.

Accustomed to these things, emerging from my woods, somewhat of a savage as I have always been, I came back from America, I opened my eyes wide and I looked for the republic. What did I see? On the highways, in the villages, on the market places, I

[9] J. J. Cart, *De la Suisse, avant la Révolution et pendant la Révolution* (Lausanne, 1802), p. 62.

saw men whose arms were adorned with green ribbons. I asked who were these men. I was told: agents of the executive. Did I belong to a republic of parrots? I despaired of the Republic. I was deeply grieved.

In the United States, of which Cart expected that, as he wrote, "before thirty years they would be in possession of Mexico, before forty of the West Indies and before fifty of the whole trade with India" everything was simple. In poor and small Switzerland, everything was far too elaborate. And still the proposal was made to emulate the American federal system! What a folly, thought Cart, who in consequence favored the strictest form of unitary administration. He wrote:

I return to my poor Switzerland and I conclude: To dress it up as the United States . . . would be to wrap up a pygmy in the garb of a giant. The trousers would be longer than the legs. He could not walk . . . The absurdity of federalizing poor little Switzerland in any way . . . is so striking . . . that I need not further dwell on the topic . . . Therefore strike out the term of canton from the Helvetic dictionary. Strike it out for ever.[10]

With less knowledge of the United States than Cart, but with the same conviction that its constitution would not suit Switzerland, Secretan, a fellow lawyer, a fellow Vaudois and a fellow Unitarian, expounded a similar anti-federalist philosophy in a pamphlet published in 1800.[11] Replying to an imaginary critic advocating, not a return to pre-revolutionary conditions but the adoption of a more enlightened form of political centralization, Secretan wrote:

. . . One may quote against my case the example of the United States of America (an example that has become very fashionable with us "exemple devenu chez nous fort à la mode").[12]—I must admit that I have never very well understood what reason should induce us to follow it. Is it perhaps the identity of our geographical position? Pray tell me what relation can there be between states spread over 300 leagues of sea coast, too far distant one from another to allow for a common administration, and our mountains

---

[10] *Ibid.*, pp. 137 ff.

[11] *Réflexions sur le fédéralisme en Helvétie*, par S. (Berne, April, 1800).

[12] I find the same expression in an anonymous article entitled "Gedanken über den Federalismus in Helvetien," published in 1801 in the *Helvetische Monatschrift*, vol. VI, p. 49. The author opposes the imitation of the United States, "now a very fashionable example" (*ein jetzt sehr modisches Beispiel*).

huddled together in a very narrow and almost circular space. Should we feel the necessity of having a President with a life tenure of office, a Stathouder or a perpetual dictator? If any of those who have suggested the American plan have felt such a need, the Helvetic people do not yet seem prepared to share their views. We have not yet discovered a Washington for us to crown.—Is it then, perhaps, that experience has shown the American government to be the best possible government? Surely a period of twenty years for a nation is but the space of its first childhood, especially if, as is the case with this nation, it has not had since its War of Independence an opportunity of testing its strength. The history of the American people has not yet been either long or memorable enough to allow one truly to judge of the excellence of its institutions.[13]

Before considering the views of the Swiss friends of these institutions, let us quote from one more of their critics. Less vivid in style than these two Vaudois, but appreciably more profound, was the Bernese professor of law Bernhard Friedrich Kuhn, since 1798 a member of the Grand Council of the Helvetic Republic. In 1800 he published a 100-page booklet on "Unity and federalism as bases for a revised Helvetic Constitution,"[14] which, in the space of a few weeks, was republished in a revised German edition[15] and shortly appeared also in French.[16]

In this very thoughtful study, Kuhn, after bitterly criticizing not only the administration of the contemporary rulers of his country, but also the unitary constitution of 1798 itself, proceeded to state the reasons why, in his opinion, the obviously unsatisfactory prevailing state of affairs did not justify a return to the former federal régime. As a loose confederation, Switzerland could not, he believed, retain her independence in the midst of the European turmoil. A unitary form of government, he claimed, was a vital national necessity. Having attacked what he denounced as "the federalism of privilege" on the one hand, and "the federalism of demagogy" on the other, he added:

[13] Secretan, *op. cit.*, pp. 15-16.

[14] *Ueber das Einheitssystem und den Föderalismus als Grundlagen einer künftigen helvetischen Staatsverfassung* (Berne, 1800).

[15] *Ibid.*, "zweyte vermehrte und verbesserte Auflage," in the first volume of *Politische Blätter*, published by Kuhn.

[16] *De l'unité et du fédéralisme considérés comme bases de la future Constitution* (Berne, 1800).

I now anticipate the objection that my criticism of a renewed federalism for Switzerland is justified only in so far as it applies to federalism in its two most extreme forms. One will say that between the two there lies a reasonable middle road, that of a federal system organized on the model of the American republic, whose national affairs are administered by a Congress which does not interfere with the independence of each allied state in its own internal administration. But has one forgotten that already at present, in its first youth, and in spite of the immense advantage it enjoys over us in that it is so far removed from the scene of the great political intrigues, it is daily becoming more aware of the disadvantages of its federal organization; and that its most enlightened statesmen consider that the only means of asserting powerfully its national independence will be completely to unite its constituent states into one unitary republic? It is well enough known how the narrow selfishness of the individual states makes impossible the execution of so many necessary, general undertakings, how it prevents the better organization of the great commercial affairs, what insuperable obstacles it places in the way of the construction of canals and highways and how it succeeded in blocking the introduction of a new financial system and the so necessary improvement of all means of general defense even at a time when the danger of a break first with England and later with France seemed imminent. All that happened in North America, although there prevails among the American people more public spirit and among the leaders of the individual states more true enlightenment than in the whole of Switzerland taken together.[17]

As these statements were vigorously challenged by his opponents, as we shall see in a moment, Kuhn declared, in a footnote in his second edition, that he based them on La Rochefoucauld-Liancourt's recent "Voyage aux Etats-Unis"[18] and on his own private conversations with "an attentive and competent observer who spent a long time in the United States in a diplomatic capacity." He added to this footnote moreover:

I do not wish to claim that the United States cannot long endure under their present constitution. The great size of their territory, the rapid increase of their population and especially the distance which separates them from Europe do not allow any comparisons between them and our small Switzerland in her extremely vulnerable position.

17 First edition; pp. 37-38.
18 F. A. F. de La Rochefoucauld-Liancourt, *Voyage dans les Etats-Unis* (Paris, 1795-1797), an VII, 8 vols.

My curiosity led me to consult Kuhn's source book, of which I was fortunate enough to find a copy in the Geneva University library. Besides much information about Philadelphia, the wealth of its citizens, the beauty of its ladies and the interests of its philosophic society,[19] which it would be tempting but unfortunately quite irrelevant to quote here, I found therein a French translation of the American federal constitution,[20] followed by some very instructive comments on its origins and on its character. These comments are hardly such as to justify Kuhn's statement. La Rochefoucauld wrote:

The knowledge I had gained of the state of affairs and of the public mind at the time of the adoption of the constituiton leads me to believe that it was the best that could then have been drafted. I shall not dwell on its principal defects, its inherent weakness which I deem to be an error in any constitution; it takes some boldness to express this view as what I believe to be a fundamental vice in the constitution of the United States is looked upon by almost all Americans as its essential virtue: I refer to its federalism.[21]

The fact is that this French nobleman, as he candidly admitted, was prejudiced against this particular characteristic of the American constitution. He loathed it because it was championed by the so-called "Anti-Federalist" party in the United States, that is, the party favorable to democracy and to the principles of the French Revolution. As he explains in his preface that he had left his country to "flee from the daggers"[22] to which his beloved cousin had succumbed in Paris, such a prejudice is assuredly as natural as it is unconvincing.

To return to Kuhn and to his Swiss associates who, in America, would have been called Federalists, that is, advocates of more federal power, we note that they alluded to the constitution of the United States only to combat its imitation in Switzerland. Some, as Cart and Secretan, argued that the American institutions were ill adapted to the very different conditions prevailing in Switzerland. Others, as Kuhn, went so far as to declare that these institutions were in themselves not

[19] *Ibid.*, vol. VI, pp. 329 *et seq.*
[20] *Ibid.*, vol. VII, pp. 159-184.
[21] *Ibid.*, vol. VII, p. 221. The author obviously takes the term of federalism in its European and not in its American sense.
[22] *Ibid.*, vol. I, p. VI.

above criticism. The very fact that even its opponents saw fit to refer to the American example shows that its friends had been very active and not unsuccessful in recommending it to the Swiss people.

These friends are to be found, not, of course, in the ranks of those extreme reactionaries whom Kuhn spoke of as "the federalists of privilege," but among careful observers of moderate views. These were equally hostile to the maintenance of the unitary republic and to the reëstablishment of the régime that had broken down in 1798. They opposed the return to the latter because it had lacked an effective central authority and because it had consecrated a system of personal and local inequality which had prevented the development of a sound national spirit.

The earliest mention of the American example in Switzerland after the revolution of 1798 I find in a letter written in May, 1799 to the historian Johann von Müller, then in Germany, by his brother-in-law in Schaffhausen. Discussing the constitutional hesitations of his country, he said: "We are of the opinion here that, with suitable modifications, it is the American constitution that would best meet our needs. There you have unity, but still each canton preserves its individuality."[23]

The next plea in favor of the American system I find in a pamphlet dated February 1st, 1800, and written by one of the countless political theologians of whom Switzerland throughout the ages seems to have produced more than her share. Under the title "Considerations on the revolution in Switzerland, on the principle of unity and indivisibility and on the necessity of returning to the federative system,"[24] J. P. Bridel, of Lausanne, writing anonymously, wrote:

The Americans have held a very different opinion on the influence and the strength inherent in federal government. At the end of the war nothing prevented them from establishing a republic one and indivisible. They did not do so. They foresaw the clashes and, measuring the practical difficulties, they sacrificed metaphysical principles to the substance of results. Although an

[23] Ed. Haug, *Der Briefwechsel der Brüder J. Georg Müller und Joh. von Müller* (Frauenfeld, 1893), vol. I, p. 175.

[24] *Réflexions sur la Révolution de la Suisse, sur le principe de l'unité et de l'indivisibilité, et sur la nécessité d'en revenir au système fédératif*, par un Suisse, du 1 Février 1800.

isolated and so to say a new people, they were divided into communities differing widely as to social standards, habits and needs. They therefore concluded that if it was useful to entrust some legislative and executive power to one national authority, it was no less useful to maintain separate local administrations and to subject to a uniform and central rule only those matters for which that was absolutely necessary in the interests of general prosperity and the defense of the Confederation. The constantly increasing prosperity which they are enjoying has justified · their policy. I salute you, brave Americans! May we, enlightened by your example, imitate your form of government![25]

In the same year another Vaudois theologian, Monneron, published what can properly be described as a political treatise. Under the title "Essay on the new political principles," Monneron, quoting Montesquieu, advocated federalism as the only means of combining individual and local freedom with national security.[26] Although federalism and political reaction had, for obvious historical reasons, come to be associated in Switzerland as in France, their association was, in his view, purely accidental and fundamentally unsound. He wrote:

Far from being associated with despotism, history shows us that federalism has always been one of its most dangerous foes. At all times federalism has been the impregnable rampart of freedom. A Mage had usurped the throne of the Persians; through federalism the monarchy was reëstablished on a more legitimate foundation. Through federalism the Greeks resisted the Romans and the Persians. Through federalism the Swiss broke the yoke of Austria. Through federalism Holland and America escaped the rule of England and Spain. Everywhere this happy combination of union against force was attended with the most complete and brilliant success.[27]

Nowhere had the federal principle been more successful than in the United States. Monneron added:

The American Confederation has in its very cradle gained a moral position which one would at first glance suppose could only be the work of a century. It has created industry, developed agriculture, encouraged manufactures, the sciences and the useful arts, repaid part of its debts; and if a destructive scourge had not some-

[25] *Ibid.*, p. 44.
[26] Frédéric Monneron, *Essai sur les nouveaux principes politiques* (Lausanne, 1800).
[27] *Ibid.*, pp. 40-41.

what slowed down the rapid pace of its prosperity, it would already have filled with inhabitants its previously desert lands.[28]

Even in Switzerland, where the former constitution "had been far from being a model of federalism," the principle had given the country 490 years of "peace and glory," whereas two years of the unitary régime had sufficed to ruin it. "Therefore," Monneron concluded, "let us base our reformed constitution on the federal principles as applied in America, eliminating the blemishes which had marred both our pre-revolutionary and our revolutionary régimes." Quoting, strangely enough, not from the federal constitution of 1789, which had been in force for over ten years, but from the discarded Articles of Confederation, Monneron urged his compatriots to adopt a balance of power between the cantons and the federal "Council of State" similar to that which had prevailed in America.[29]

This ignorance of the actual state of American constitutional law, indeed surprising in the author of an important work on federalism published in 1800, confirms us in the impression that the American model was more admired than studied and understood in many Swiss quarters. One knew that the United States were neither a mere alliance of local sovereignties, such as Switzerland had been before 1798, nor a unitary state, such as it had become then. One knew, also, that the United States were as happy and prosperous as Switzerland was discontented and miserable. Therefore, many concluded, let us copy the American model!

The protests aroused by Kuhn's statement to the effect that the Americans themselves were dissatisfied with their constitution do not seem to have been based on much better authority than the statement itself.

Thus F. R. Lerber, a member of the former Bernese legislature, in a pamphlet printed in May 1800, that is, immediately after the publication of Kuhn's attack, wrote:

One claims that the North American Constitution has already revealed the disadvantages of the federal system; according to the accounts of travellers which are known to me, this is an entirely new complaint. Rather should I attribute the difficulties which have sometimes arisen to the passion for change and the unstable principles which the daily flood of new immigrants from all corners of

[28] *Ibid.*, p. 47.
[29] *Ibid.*, pp. 97 *et seq.*

the earth, of adventurers fleeing all ordered conditions and seeking fortune in all ways naturally brings with it and also to the unlimited democracy which prevails in certain states. And if the recent reports are true, one is doubtless busy abroad combating the evils in question.[30]

A similar, equally lame refutation of Kuhn's statements is to be found in another German-Swiss pamphlet written in June 1800 and published anonymously and without any indication of place of publication in 1801. The author, after arguing on general principles in favor of a fair and liberal distribution of power between the central and local authorities, proceeded:

As for the practicability of such an organization, it is irrefutably demonstrated not only by many ancient constitutions, but also by the recent North American Union of States. The friends of a unitary state may invent against this fact whatever fables they please. One fails to see why the same force which has founded the united republics should not, under similar circumstances, be able to maintain them.[31]

In a footnote the author added:

The friends of unity undeservedly defame the North American States. They claim that their most enlightened statesmen also desire to merge them all into one unit.

This statement has often been challenged as being without foundation. The wishes of a few dreamers are rarely those of a reasonable nation which cherishes its welfare. That the Americans have not desired such a fusion is best shown by the fact that they have never discussed it.—According to all probabilities, the increasing population of their states will lead to secessions rather than to unification.

The same somewhat superficial and uncritical enthusiasm for the American system was displayed by J. F. Armand in a pamphlet entitled "Tribute to my fatherland, or sketch of a draft constitution of the Helvetic Republic based on the sovereignty of the cantons." He wrote:

Everyone knows that the United States of America possess all the attributes and rights of sovereignty, that they delegate a part

---

[30] F. R. Lerber, *Betrachtungen zum Vortheil des Bundes-Systems oder Föderalismus für die Schweiz*, Berne, 1800, p. 51.

[31] *Prüfung der Gründe für und wider das Einheits-System und den Föderalismus in der Schweiz* (1801), pp. 47-48.

thereof to a Congress entrusted with the administration of diplomatic and military affairs and that under the auspices of this
happy constitution their population and their prosperity are most
brilliantly increasing day by day.[32]

These various quotations, which it would be more fastidious
than impossible to multiply by further research, suffice to show
both the importance of the American precedent in the Swiss
constitutional debates at the beginning of the last century and
the lack of precise information then prevailing about it in
Switzerland.[33] The authors are obviously advocates and not
scholars. As most advocates, they are more intent on making
their points than enlightened about the facts adduced in support of them. Even if they seem less convincing than they were
themselves convinced, this constant reiteration of the American argument was certainly significant and not without effect.

Thus in the correspondence of the Burgomaster of Basle,
who was representing his canton in the Federal Diet in Berne,
we find a letter dated September 11, 1802, in which he wrote:

I know very well that the unitary system does not suit our people
and I shall certainly miss no opportunity to endeavor to modify
our constitution so as to render it as similar as possible to that of
the United States of America.[34]

Still more significant as a proof of the influence exerted by
the American precedent on the constitutional evolution of
Switzerland is the following: The various drafts considered
between 1801 and 1803 were all more or less inspired by the
French First Consul himself, then the supreme legislator of
Europe, as great military conquerors are apt to become. Now,
we have it on the evidence of the Swiss Minister in Paris,

[32] J. F. Armand, *Hommage à ma patrie, ou Esquisse d'un projet de constitution de la République Helvétique, fondé sur la souveraineté des cantons'*
(Neuchâtel, 1801), pp. 27-28.

[33] In spite of the many allusions to the institutions of the United States
occurring in the Swiss literature of this period, we have not noted a single
precise bibliographical reference to any American or even to any European work
on the subject except that of La Rochefoucauld. Neither the *Federalist*, nor
John Adams' *A Defence of the Constitution of Government of the United
States*, of both of which there had appeared French translations in Paris in
1792, seems to have been read in Switzerland. A man who was later to become
one of Geneva's most prominent citizens had, in 1795, published two volumes
on the United States, in which a French translation of the constitution of
1789 is also to be found: C. Pictet, *Tableau de la situation actuelle des Etats-
Unis d'Amérique*, 2 vols (Paris, 1795).

[34] Karl Wieland, *Briefe von Bürgermeister Johann Karl Wieland aus den
Jahren 1797-1803. Beiträge zur vaterl. Geschichte*, vol. VI, p. 139.

Stapfer, that Bonaparte favored the American precedent for Switzerland. Stapfer's reports are all the more convincing on this point as he, being a firm Unitarian, could not but deplore the advice they conveyed. Writing to the Swiss Foreign Minister, Louis Bégos, on October 8, 1800, Stapfer said:

Bonaparte has recently expressed the opinion that it would be suitable for Switzerland to constitute herself into a few important states bound together by a tie such as that of the American Congress (sic) and Senate.[35]

A few months later, on February 23, 1801, Stapfer, in another dispatch to his home government, wrote:

I had a conference yesterday with the Councillor of State Roederer, whose opinion is of great importance. He assured me that the ideas of the First Consul were not yet entirely fixed, but that he was inclined to favor a constitution on the American model.[36]

The so-called Act of Mediation of 1803, under which Switzerland lived in surprising quiet and contentment throughout the Napoleonic wars, was drafted, if not by the French dictator, at least under his immediate influence. Although in appearance very different from the American constitution of 1789, it was indeed far less so than the Helvetic constitution of 1798 which it replaced. Whereas, under the latter, Switzerland had known a bicameral legislature, one house intended to represent the cantons and the other their population, the Act of Mediation revived the traditional Swiss unicameral Diet. In fact, however, under the régime of the Act of Mediation of 1803 the distribution of power between the national and the local authorities was very similar to that provided for under the American constitution. The cantons, which had lost all autonomy in 1798, were set up again as truly self-governing units and the powers of the reëstablished federal Diet were far more limited than had been those of the central authorities under the constitution of the one and indivisible Republic. The federal government, it is true, was in 1803 endowed with appreciably more authority than it had enjoyed before 1798 and the Act provided for the novel position of Landammann of Switzerland, the closest approach to an American President in the constitutional annals of the country. Thus the Act of Mediation of

[35] Strickler, op. cit., vol. VI (Berne, 1897), p. 260.
[36] Ibid., vol. VI, p. 721.

1803 made of Switzerland, for the first time in its history, a truly federal state on the American model.

THE RESTORATION, 1814-1830

From 1803, when it came into force, until 1830, when the first democratic revolutions broke out in the principal cantons, Switzerland knew no more violent constitutional debates. From 1803 to 1813, the will of Napoleon was supreme. In 1814, with his downfall, began a period of political reaction. During this period the Swiss people were hardly more their own masters, but it was no longer Paris, but Vienna that called the tune.

Under the Federal Pact of 1815, which was drafted under the influence and indeed under the pressure of the Allied Powers, the sovereignty of the cantons was almost entirely reëstablished, the constitutional bond uniting them loosened almost to the point at which the Helvetic Republic had found it in 1798, and the privileged position of the formerly ruling families almost completely restored in fact if not in law.

As Bonaparte in 1803, his victors in 1814 wished to see an orderly Switzerland, but not a strongly unified one that might be tempted to pursue an active foreign policy. On April 21st, 1814, while the federal Diet was engaged in the laborious task of framing a new constitution, it received a memorandum from the Allied diplomats, who were watching and guiding its labors. After urging the Swiss legislators to seek salvation in "a strong federal bond," stronger than the extremists among the reactionary cantons would have forged it if left to their own devices, they added:

This strength cannot be found in a central authority and could in no case result from its creation. America, which presents an example of such an institution, has nothing in common with Switzerland. To understand it, one has only to consider the respective origins, internal relations and external circumstances of the two confederations.

Switzerland is neutral by her very essence. Her neutrality must be founded on an unshakable and imposing inertia (*une inébranlable et imposante inertie*.[37]

[37] *Abschied* der am 6. April 1814 zu Zürich versammelten und am 31. August 1815 daselbst geschlossenen ausserordentlichen eidgenössischen Tagsatzung, vol. I, Beilage Litt. F., p. 2.

Arguing in favor of a more strongly organized federal state, in a pamphlet published about the same time, Rengger, on the contrary, wrote: "We do not demand a stronger federal union than that which has made a nation of the Dutch and of the Americans."[38]

Thus, even during the triumphant reaction of 1814, the American example was constantly before the eyes of the Swiss. But the scene had completely shifted. This alone and not a change of personal conviction explains how Rengger, who formerly repudiated the American model as insufficiently "unitarian" now came to invoke it in favor of his case. He now argued that the least he could demand for Switzerland was that measure of unity which the American constitution had secured for the United States.

The spirit of the age, however, as represented by the Holy Alliance without and by the Swiss reactionaries within, was as hostile to any form of national centralization as it was to internal politcal liberty. Accordingly, under the Federal Pact, which finally came into force on August 7, 1815, the great body of the people were debarred from all political activity. The federal Diet, which was set up as the supreme authority in the Confederation, was made up of plenipotentiaries bound by the instructions of their respective cantons each of which could cast only one vote. As further more constant pressure from without, combined with a strict censorship within, seriously limited the freedom of speech and of the press, there was, at the beginning of the Restoration period, no public platform for constitutional discussions in Switzerland.

These broke out again in 1830, however, with all the more ardor, as they had long been repressed. When the July revolution in Paris showed Europe and the world that the much feared Holy Alliance was unable or unwilling to maintain by force the institutions that had been set up under its preponderant influence in 1815, the Swiss people hastened to make the most of their newly discovered freedom.

In fact, even in the last years preceding 1830, individual voices had been heard here and there denouncing the existing governments as unrepresentative of the people, and the Federal Pact of 1815 as contrary to their national ideals. More freedom

[38] *Dr. Albrecht Renggers kleine ungedruckte Schriften*, ed. by Kortüm, Berne, 1838, p. 208.

within the cantons and closer union between them in the
Confederation, such was the cry raised by private citizens here
and there and loudly applauded by the masses whenever circumstances allowed them to display their feelings. Travelling
through Switzerland in the summer of 1828, the American
novelist Fenimore Cooper noted that "all the liberal and enlightened Swiss . . . admit that the present system is imper-
fect." He added:

> Most of them, it is true, are opposed to consolidation, for the
> inhabitants of the towns object to having their policy brought
> down to the level of that of the mountaineers; but they desire a
> Union like our own, in place of the Confederation,—a central
> government, that for certain common objects, can act directly on
> the people, without the interference of agents, who derive their
> authority from a different source.[39]

One of the most active centers of Swiss political thought
during the dark period of the Restoration was the Helvetic
Society. This private organization, grouping public-spirited
citizens from all parts of the country, had been founded in
1761. With brief interruptions, from 1798 to 1807 and from
1814 to 1819, when the political situation prevented it, they had
met every year freely to talk over among themselves matters
of common patriotic interest. After 1819, their main topic of
discussion was the very one which had led to their first gathering, towards the end of the prerevolutionary régime, namely,
the unsatisfactory character of the relations between the sovereign cantons and the generally felt desire to strengthen the
bonds between them. This inevitably led them to consider the
need for, and possibilities of, federal constitutional reform.

At the two last meetings of the Helvetic Society before the
revolution of 1830, the tone and substance of the speeches delivered were particularly significant in this connection.

On May 12, 1829, their venerable president, the historian
Heinrich Zschokke, who had already in 1824, in a pamphlet,
denounced the national peril of the prevailing intercantonal
anarchy,[40] and who had long been a great admirer of America,[41]

---

[39] J. Fenimore Cooper, *Excursions in Switzerland* (Paris, 1836), p. 154.

[40] Heinrich Zschokke, *Betrachtung einer grossen Angelegenheit des eids-
genössischen Vaterlandes* (Aarau, 1824).

[41] In 1818 he had published an article entitled *"Europa's Niedergang
Amerika's Aufgang"* (Europa's fall America's rise) of which the final words in-

devoted his opening address to the distressing state of the Republic. Ever since 1814, he showed, the nation had moved in one direction and the state in another. The people were ever more eager for political freedom and national unity, whereas their authorities were sternly repressive and insistent on the principle of absolute cantonal sovereignty. Zschokke pointed out how the Federal Pact of 1815 contributed to this state of affairs by saying:

As the Federal Pact, with hardly a restriction, allowed the majesty of the whole Confederation to be buried in the grave of the absolute sovereignty of twenty-two local administrations, the federal Diet itself inevitably fell to the level of an exchange market for the negotiation of twenty-two local interests. Each canton, as indeed it must, there raises its voice only to defend its own needs against those of its neighbors. But who then speaks for the Confederation as a whole against the various cantons? Who then defends the honor, the welfare and the might of the Swiss nation? The parts decide for the whole, because they are more than the whole and because they constitute a league of states and not a federal state.[42]

Zschokke concluded his impassioned oration in the following terms:

Truly, if the Swiss citizen must forget Switzerland and, limiting his loyalty to his local home, become insensitive to the pain of his bleeding patriotism, then it would be better to strike out the divine classics from the curriculum of our schools and to blot out in the minds of our children the memories of the heroes of ancient Greece and Rome, and indeed also those of Washington, Franklin, Jefferson and the other immortal citizens of the American federal state.[43]

Thus we again see how, whereas under the unitary régime of 1798 the American example had been pointed to as a model by the conservative federalists, under the reactionary constitution of 1815 it became the inspiration of the liberal, forward-looking national patriots.

dicate the general inspiration. They were: "From now on America shall be the home of human culture and the light-house of the globe, towards which the individual sages in all countries will look with yearning and grateful blessings." H. Zschokke's *ausgewählte Schriften*, vol X (Aarau, 1825), p. 322.

[42] *Verhandlungen der Helvetischen Gesellschaft zu Schinznach im Jahr 1829* (Zurich), pp. 34-35.

[43] *Ibid.*, p. 42.

At the next meeting of the Helvetic Society, in May 1830, Dr. Schinz, a member of the Supreme Court of Zurich, having declared that the liberal and more numerous part of the Swiss people had lost all confidence in their governments and, after denouncing the Federal Pact of 1815 as a "political bastard," went on to make the following statement, which I quote literally for reasons which no American reader will fail to understand: "All the governments of Switzerland must become aware of the fact that they are but governments of the people, by the people and for the people."[44]

These words, uttered a full generation before the delivery of Lincoln's Gettysburg address, may help to explain why the thought of the American people and the example of their constitutional arrangements were ever in the minds of their Swiss fellow democrats.

THE "REGENERATION," 1830-1833

With the local revolutions of 1830, which endowed all the leading Swiss cantons with liberal institutions and popularly elected legislatures, there begins the second period of active discussion in Switzerland of American bicameral federalism. This discussion was to be carried on simultaneously on two distinct planes, on the one hand, in privately printed pamphlets and newspaper articles and in speeches delivered at unofficial gatherings. In these the American constitution was closely studied and the adoption in Switzerland, first of its federal principles and later also of its bicameral system, openly and frankly urged by an enthusiastic group of democratic reformers. On the other hand, on March 25, 1831, the government of Thurgau, one of the recently revolutionized cantons, officially proposed that all cantons be invited to instruct their delegates to the federal Diet to consider "the ways and means of revising the Swiss federal constitution in order to bring about a stronger centralization in the superior interests of Switzerland as a whole."

That the private and the public discussions thus launched sprang from one and the same source is certain. Thomas Born-

44 "Alle Regierungen der Schweiz müssen es erkennen, dass sie blos aus dem Volke, durch das Volk und für das Volk da sind." Karl Morell, *Die helvetische Gesellschaft* (Winterthur, 1863), p. 398.

hauser, a poetically gifted and politically minded Protestant pastor, the principal leader in the cantonal revolution of 1830 in Thurgau[45] and the principal inspirer of the official invitation addressed by his government to the other cantons in 1831,[46] was also a convinced believer in the American constitutional principles and an active promoter of their adoption in Switzerland.[47]

Moreover it is significant that a German translation of the American constitution was published in Frauenfeld, the capital of Thurgau, in 1831, with the following mention printed on the title page: "recommended to the attention of the Swiss citizens on the occasion of the revision of their federal pact."[48]

Furthermore G. Baumgartner, of Saint-Gall, and Casimir Pfyffer, of Lucerne, were, as we shall see presently, both among the first and most prominent leaders of the popular movement in favor of an Americanized federal constitution and they were also actively engaged in promoting the revision of the Pact of 1815 by the federal Diet.

But although the original link between the private and the official debates on constitutional reform from 1831 onwards is thus well established, the tone of the one and of the other were very different and their tendencies were, from the start, clearly divergent.

Let us therefore examine each in turn, beginning with the unofficial discussions which preceded and suggested the official debates, but whose more extreme leaders were soon to combat the latter's conclusions.

The first reference to the American constitution as a model for Switzerland that was made after the July revolutions of 1830 and before the organized agitation in its favor throughout the country, was apparently to be found in a petition drafted in Paris in the latter half of 1830. The authors, who seem to have remained anonymous, were a group of higher Swiss officers serving in the so-called "capitulated" Swiss regiments in France. These officers, with their troops, had been summarily dismissed when the régime of Louis Philippe triumphed over that

[45] J. Christinger, *Thomas Bornhauser* (Frauenfeld, 1875), pp. 90 *et seq.*
[46] *Ibid.*, p. 158.
[47] *Ibid.*, pp. 159 *et seq.*
[48] *Constitution der Vereinigten Staaten von Nordamerika.* "Der Aufmerksamkeit der Eidgenossen empfohlen bei Anlass der Revision ihrer Bunder-Akte," 24 pages (Frauenfeld, 1831).

of Charles X which, under their military oath of allegiance to the French crown, they had been bound to defend. They had at the same time been deprived of the rights granted to them by international treaty.[49] Having in vain appealed to the Swiss authorities in what they deemed to be not only a matter of personal justice but also of national dignity, they appear thereby to have been led to the belief that only a radical reform of the federal structure of their country could restore its international standing.

Unfortunately I have as yet been unable to discover a copy of this publication which, when I undertook this study, had been entirely forgotten. In spite of repeated searching investigations in libraries and archives in Geneva, in Berne, in Fribourg and elsewhere, investigations in which I have been most diligently and intelligently assisted by various fellow-scholars,[50] none has yet been found. My knowledge of it was, therefore, at first based only on secondary sources. These, however, were sufficiently clear and concordant to justify further research.

The most authoritative mention of the matter, that to which all subsequent authors refer, is to be found in the four volume history of the Swiss revolutions from 1830 to 1848 of J. Baumgartner, the above-mentioned statesman from Saint-Gall. The relevant passage, which I translate from the original German, reads as follows:

Strangely enough, the procession of thousands of petitioners and reformers interested in a new federal order was opened by defenders of Charles X in Paris, higher staff officers in the disbanded Swiss regiments there. In strong language they demanded a real federal government similar to that of the United States of North America. 'Modify their federal constitution as you wish, omit from it or add to it what you think fit. But give us that national force which can come only from the closest union.' A draft of the new federal constitution on quite centralized lines, which was printed in Geneva, lent the necessary formal expression to the wishes and views of these petitioners. But their draft was ill-received both in the west and in the east of the country. The principal reason for this disfavor was probably to be found in the fact that the project was the work of men who had devoted their spiritual and physical forces to foreign service abroad and who therefore

[49] Cf. Jean-Charles Biaudet, *La fin des capitulations avec la France, 1830*, Zeitschrift für Schweizerische Geschichte (Zurich, 1940), pp. 98-127.

[50] My particular thanks are due to M. Marcel Godet, director of the federal library and to Professor Kern, director of the federal archives, both in Berne.

had had the least opportunity of becoming familiar with conditions in Switzerland. Indeed, friends of the reform movement suspected their intention of setting up a central government on the basis of military power, a dictatorship such as were then prevalent in parts of South America and in Poland . . . In the authorship of this immature production Philip de Maillardoz from Fribourg and Augustus de Bontems from Geneva, two officers who were later colonels in the Swiss federal army, had participated.[51]

Another more immediately contemporaneous reference to this plan is to be found in a pamphlet published in Geneva in July 1831 by a liberal member of the cantonal legislature.[52] In this pamphlet, containing a critical review of the "demands for revision of the Swiss Federal Pact which have been raised in various quarters," we read:

The first of these petitions, the earliest and the one which has given rise to all the others, dates from November 1830; it was drafted and printed in Paris by the superior officers of the "capitulated" regiments and from there it was distributed all over the country.

This is a summary of the plan there suggested.

The federal political authorities would consist of:

A President chosen by the Diet from a list of candidates presented by the cantons.

Four "Landammanns" chosen by four parts of Switzerland, from the north, the south, the west and the center, each of which would choose one.

A Diet, composed of deputies two for each section of 50,000 inhabitants and less, and one for each additional section of 50,000 inhabitants. On this basis, its composition would be as follows:

Berne	7	Lucerne	3
Zurich	4	Saint-Gall	3
Vaud	4	Ticino	3
Aargau	4		

These 7 cantons would thus supply	28	deputies
and the 15 others, each two	30	"
Making a total of	58	" [53]

---

[51] J. Baumgartner, *Die Schweiz in ihren Kämpfen und Umgestaltungen von 1830 bis 1850*, vol. I (Zurich, 1853), pp. 162 *et seq.*

[52] Fazy-Pasteur (Député au Conseil représentatif du Canton de Genève), *Observations sur les changements demandés au Pacte fédéral helvétique* (Geneva, 1831).

[53] *Ibid.*, p. 15.

Having examined a series of other plans, to which we shall revert presently, Fazy-Pasteur added: "In examining the proposed draft changes, one observes that they are obviously all more or less absolutely based on the constitution of the United States of America."[54]

Let me quote one more final contemporaneous allusion to the suggestion of the Swiss officers in Paris. I find it in the first volume of the *Swiss Annals or History of our Times since July 1830*[55] published by a former Landammann of Saint-Gall who retired from office after the revolution in his canton. This disgruntled magistrate, in words that will amuse American readers, thus opposes isolationist Switzerland and imperialist America:

In the last days of the year 1830 . . . two appeals signed by many very honorable Swiss residing in Paris were circulated, proposing the establishment of a central government on the model of the American free state. No one doubted the sincere intentions of their authors any more than their absolute ignorance of conditions in their fatherland. What has Switzerland in common with North America, with its vast area and its large affairs, the habits and character of its inhabitants? How can one draw a parallel between Switzerland, whose destiny it is to pursue a wise, moderate, harmonious policy of isolation, and the mighty nation which throws itself into all world conflicts and makes itself respected in all parts of the globe by the force of its arms?[56]

When I started on my quest for further information, the only other indication of the contents of this highly interesting (but unfortunately lost) plan of the Swiss officers in Paris, I discovered in some other of the pamphlets referred to by Fazy-Pasteur. Several of these had been published by other officers in Geneva in the first half of 1831, probably under the influence of the French precedent.

Thus, in one of these pamphlets bearing the signature of L. Rilliet,[57] who had also taken service in France under Napoleon and then under Louis XVIII, we read:

[54] *Ibid.*, p. 34.

[55] Carl Müller von Friedberg, *Schweizerische Annalen oder die Geschichte unserer Tage seit dem Julius 1830* (Zurich, 1832).

[56] *Ibid.*, pp. 216, 217.

[57] L. Rilliet, *Nouvelles observations sur le service suisse capitulé* (Geneva, 1831).

In 1830, the Swiss [in France] are overwhelmed by an unheard-of revolution, sacrificed without purpose and without reason and finally brusquely discharged by the victorious party . . . On learning of these events the Diet adjourns.

Listen to its motives.

The Diet is a body which can have no opinion, no will of its own. It is but the organ of twenty-two sovereign wills . . .

I do not believe the Federal Pact to be a perfect instrument. I believe the friends of Switzerland should wish that it should soon be appreciably amended. . . . But does anyone think that if the Diet had formulated an immediate protest at once firm and moderate in favor of the Swiss regiments, it would have offended against the spirit of the Federal Pact?[58]

Although this pamphlet contains no express mention of the American example, I have quoted it because it explains the position as seen by military men in Switzerland at the time. Swiss soldiers have been unjustly treated abroad by a foreign government. The Swiss authorities are unable or unwilling to secure redress. Therefore the Swiss constitution must be amended to strengthen their hand for the future.

The same general view was put forward by another Swiss officer, A. Roger, a major in the Swiss federal engineers. In a pamphlet also published in the spring of 1831,[59] he wrote:

When North America shook off the yoke of England, it remained a prey to disunion and to the selfishness of the individual states of the federation. It took no less than the persistent efforts and the great prestige of Washington during ten years to overcome these difficulties.

However, Washington was not a genius. He was something more, an excellent citizen who sought glory in establishing the happiness of his country on a solid foundation and this glory will last to the most remote posterity.[60]

After this preamble Roger, in his pamphlet, submitted a revised-draft constitution for Switzerland in which the American influence would be obvious even if it were not expressly recognized. After suggesting the popular election of a president for a term of six years, with the provision that no one could serve two successive terms, he added:

[58] *Ibid.*, pp. 3, 4.
[59] A. Roger, *Essai sur le lien fédéral en Suisse* (Geneva, 1831).
[60] *Ibid.*, p. 7.

Let him [the Swiss president] have constantly before his eyes the noble example of Washington and Franklin, whose ardent and enlightened patriotism has won for them a glory greater than that of all the glories of the world and one which will last until the end of time.[61]

This pamphlet was reviewed, on April 14, 1831, in the *Journal de Genève*, then the organ of the local liberal opposition. The commentator wrote:

Many excellent citizens have often sighed over the kind of oscillations which characterize the political system of the Helvetic Republic. Several writings have been published on the important topic. But one is forced to admit that until now one has been content to dismiss such ideas as Utopian. Will Mr. Roger be more fortunate than his predecessors? One may doubt it, so powerful is the influence of habit and of routine, so effectively do special interests oppose the common good.[62]

We now have before us a complete picture of the position of military circles in Switzerland on the question of constitutional reform in 1830. But we still have no precise knowledge of the contents of the petition and of the draft constitution referred to in the contemporary writings we have quoted. Where are these documents to be found and why have they disappeared? That is the question I could not but put to myself and to all those whose expert knowledge was, thanks to their kindness, at my disposal.

In order to explain this otherwise entirely inexplicable disappearance, I was tempted to believe that it was willed by its victims. As we shall see presently, the adaptation to Swiss conditions of American constitutional principles was shortly to become one of the main planks in the platform of the Swiss radical extremists. Now Maillardoz, Bontemps and many other staff officers formerly in French service, soon took high rank in the Swiss federal army. By reason of this circumstance and of their birth and social position, they were naturally all staunch conservatives. May one not, therefore, surmise that they soon deplored their past attitude on the American issue and accord-

---

[61] *Ibid.*, pp. 24 *et seq.*

[62] *Journal de Genève*, April 14, 1831, p. 66. Of other pamphlets see also F. Bordier, *Améliorations militaires et administratives, ayant pour but d'augmenter les forces de la Suisse pour la défense de sa neutralité* (Geneva, 1831).

ingly left no stone unturned in order to suppress all trace
of it?[63]

In any case I knew that in the latter half of 1830 Maillardoz
represented the Diet in its negotiations with the French government over the pension rights of the dismissed troops, and
that he and Bontemps became officers in the Swiss federal army
in 1831.

Did this not offer a clue? Through my colleague, Professor
Kern of Berne, my attention was drawn to some manuscript
letters received by Maillardoz in the last months of 1830 from
various correspondents. These letters, relating mainly to military affairs, had been lying for years unclassified and uncon-
sulted in the federal archives.

To my delight, I discovered therein several explicit references both to the petition and also to the above-mentioned draft
constitution. It would take us too far afield were we here to
analyze this correspondence which I hope some day to publish
elsewhere. Suffice it to say that its perusal led me, if not yet
to discover the original documents in question, at least to
ascertain the exact and complete contents of the petition and
to know how and why Maillardoz who had drafted it came
to drop the matter. The correspondence shows also that Bontemps, who, from the start, had doubts about the wisdom of
the petition, supplemented it by the publication, in Basançon
or Geneva, of a draft constitution. As for the contents of the
latter document, in which he also very shortly lost all interest
for the above alleged reasons, and which is still undiscovered,
we can judge of it only by the analysis published by Fazy-
Pasteur and quoted above.

The text of the petition I finally found reprinted, *in extenso*, in the *Journal de Genève* of December 23, 1830. Addressed to the "magistrates of all the cantons," it contains the
following passage:

[63] M. Pierre de Zurich, a well-known historian of Fribourg, has done me
the great favor of searching for this mysterious pamphlet through all the very
rich libraries and archives of his native town, which was also the home of
Maillardoz. The only fact at all relevant to the present research, he was able to
discover, was the publication by the same Maillardoz in 1838 of a 6 page
pamphlet entitled: "An essay on the revision of one article of the Federal
Pact" (Essai sur la révision d'un article du Pacte Fédéral, Fribourg, 1838).
The pamphlet contains no mention of any previous writings by the author on
the same subject, nor any reference to the American precedent.

A government similar to that of the United States of America would suit our ancient confederation just as well as it suits those young and wise republics; modify their federal constitution as you wish, omit from it or add to it what you think fit, but give us that national force which can come only from the closest union.[64]

The document was subjected by the editors of the *Journal de Genève* to a very bitter criticism.[65]

They wrote:

This insidious petition tends to nothing less, as we read it, than to set up a dictatorial government and thus to destroy our cantonal sovereignty . . . We also believe in the necessity of a revision of the federal pact . . . but we believe that a presidential office such as that of the United States of America would in no way suit Switzerland.

Thus it appears that in 1830, conservative Swiss officers were attracted to the American constitution by the very feature which most displeased those of its radical friends in Switzerland who were about to agitate for its imitation on other grounds.

After this brief military interlude or rather prelude, that campaign soon started with some vigor. During the years 1830 and 1831, its general aims did not go beyond the transformation of the Swiss Confederation into a federal state. The model its leaders had before their eyes was both the Swiss Act of Mediation of 1803 and the American constitution of 1789. But of the latter they at first invoked not its bicameralism, but only those of its provisions which had resulted in the setting up of the "more perfect union." They expressly discarded any idea of a unitary state, such as had been the ill-starred Helvetic Republic, the generally abhorred memory of which was constantly being evoked by the conservatives as a bugbear. But they wished to extend the powers of the confederation and to transform the Diet from an assembly of plenipotentiaries into a true parliament, by freeing its members from written instructions and by departing from the rule of equal representation of unequal cantons.

The first announcement of this policy to be made public in

[64] *Loc. cit.*, p. 214.

[65] It was to this criticism and to the grief it gave Maillardoz who complained of it to its correspondents that I owe my good fortune in finding the document in the *Journal de Genève*.

Switzerland by a prominent Swiss politician was the "appeal to the federal Vorort of Lucerne on the occasion of its assumption of the administration of federal affairs on New Year's Day 1831" by Dr. Casimir Pfyffer, of Lucerne.[66]

The publication of this pamphlet was an event of national importance. Under the Pact of 1815, Lucerne was, with Zurich and Berne, one of the three "directing" cantons whose governments were in turn responsible for the administration of national affairs while the Diet was not sitting. As the only Catholic canton of the three, Lucerne was the natural leader of the confessional minority of the country. On the very eve of her assumption of the "directorship" for the two following years, she had undergone a democratic constitutional revision. This had placed her in the camp of the so-called "regenerated" cantons, which had substituted liberal representative institutions for the aristocratic régime prevailing since 1814. Moreover Casimir Pfyffer, although belonging to an old aristocratic family, had been one of the leaders of the democratic movement. In spite of his youth—he was born in 1794—he had been elected to the Grand Council in 1826 and had been Lucerne's second delegate to the federal Diet in 1828.

That a man in such a position should, under such circumstances, in a published pamphlet, address an appeal to the government of his canton was in itself unusual. Still more so was the substance of the appeal itself.

Pfyffer therein did no less than propose a new federal constitution and call upon his canton to assume "the great and magnificent task, as Vorort, of initiating the revision of the Federal Pact."[67] The new constitution, of which the main principles were outlined in the pamphlet, was to provide for a federal state in which a so-called "Federal Council" was to be substituted, as a representative legislature, for the existing Diet. The members of this parliament were to be elected by the cantonal legislatures for a term of several years. They were not, as heretofore the delegates to the Diet were, to be bound by instructions and each to cast only one cantonal vote.

---

[66] "Zuruf an den eidgenössischen Vorort Luzern bei Uebernahme der Leitung der Bundes-Angelegenheiten auf das Neujahr 1831." Quoted from *Sammlung einiger kleineren Schriften Dr. Kasimir Pfyffers* . . . (Lucerne, 1866), pp. 31 et seq.

[67] *Ibid.*, p. 40.

They were to speak and to vote as free representatives of the cantonal electorates, each of which was to have a number of members proportional to its size. As the Federal Council was to be the supreme legislative authority, and as its decisions were to be taken by majority votes, the adoption of Pfyffer's scheme would have implied the abolition of cantonal sovereignty. Furthermore, the proposed federal constitution was expressly to be based upon the principle of popular sovereignty, of liberty and equality, of republican democratic representative institutions, of the freedom of establishment and the freedom of the press and it was to ensure the general enforcement of these principles throughout the land.[68]

Although the appeal does not expressly refer to the American precedent, it was clearly inspired by it. Its author was therefore fully justified when, addressing the Grand Council of Lucerne as its president, on September 14, 1848, on the morrow of the adoption of the new Swiss constitution on the American model, he declared: "I rejoice in the thought that I was the first, in January 1831, to give expression to the wish then already cherished in many hearts that our federal institutions be reformed."[69]

When Casimir Pfyffer published his memorable appeal, he was doubtless voicing the hopes of many. But if he believed that these hopes were shared by an overwhelming majority of his compatriots and that they would therefore promptly be realized, he was grievously mistaken. Already the venerable H. Zschokke, to whom he had previously sent for publication an article on the same topic, had replied, in November 1830:

You will allow me to keep and to spare until the proper time your essay on the reform of the federal constitution. Today, when everybody is actively engrossed in reforming cantonal constitutions, the plea for something more general would pass unheeded.[70]

Soon realizing that Swiss public opinion was as yet neither sufficiently enlightened nor sufficiently aroused to impose any bold action upon the traditionally conservative Diet, Pfyffer and his friends seized every opportunity to enlighten and to arouse it. In May 1831, Pfyffer addressed the Helvetic Society

[68] Ibid., pp. 41 et seq.
[69] Pfyffer, Sammlung, etc., op. cit., p. 136.
[70] Ibid., p. 283.

on the subject,[71] and on September 25, 1831, there met at his invitation, at Langenthal, in the canton of Berne, reformers from nine cantons and founded there the so-called "Swiss Security Society."[72] The main purpose of this organization, which was soon to found branches in several other cantons, was to protect the cantonal democratic constitutions against all reactionary movements. But it also, in its statutes, stated among its aims, "the preparation, for a time which will be deemed favorable, of a revision of the Federal Pact." And we have it on Pfyffer's own authority that, for him at least, that was the essential aim of the organization.[73]

Although the American example does not seem to have been expressly mentioned at these gatherings, it is not irrelevant to our purpose to recall them here. They undoubtedly served to promote the cause of the federalizing of Switzerland and furthermore they appear to have been the first occasion on which such men as Münzinger of Solothurn, Oertli of Appenzell, and Druey of Lausanne, who in 1848 were among the framers of the revised bicameral constitution, met to exchange their views on the subject.

Besides these widely reported public meetings, the reformers also seem to have promoted their plans by writing or inspiring articles in the press. In these, a much bolder language was spoken. Thus, for instance, there appeared anonymously, in the *Journal de Genève*, on September 15, 1831,[74] four columns on the "Revision of the Federal Pact." In this article the framers of the Pact of 1815 were blamed for not creating "a second chamber, in which the Swiss population would have been directly represented, whereas the Diet maintained as it is would, under the name of Senate or first Chamber, have stood for the cantonal interests." The anonymous author added:

Under the present federal Pact there are questions of the first importance which may not even be mentioned, so great is the fear

---

[71] *Ibid.*, pp. 61 *et seq.*

[72] *Ibid.*, pp. 281 *et seq.*; Baumgartner, *op. cit.*, vol. I, p. 169; J. L. B. Leresche, *Biographie politique de Henri Druey* (Lausanne, 1857), p. 66.

[73] Cf. *Journal de Genève*, December 15, 1831, p. 223; Baumgartner, *op. cit.*, vol. I, p. 262.

[74] P. 163. This article has never, to my knowledge, been attributed to James Fazy. There would seem to be no doubt, however, that he was its author, as it constitutes the first part of an undated pamphlet he published some months or years later. Cf. p. 86.

that by mentioning them one might offend the prejudices rooted in the minds of some cantonal governments. . . . Switzerland needs a central government in which all these inhibitions could be overcome by persuasion and in which a real, ardent interest could be aroused in national affairs. The federal system of the United States of America is the only one which fulfills these conditions: in the course of the last fifty years, during which it has been in operation, it has been instrumental in harmonizing all the conflicting interests and in organizing a powerful central government so that it has never become necessary to have recourse to arms to constrain the constituent states. This is all the more remarkable as the interests of the latter are still more complex and more diverse than those of our cantons.

Such anonymous articles, as also the anonymous publication of the German translation of the American constitution in Thurgau in the same year 1831, already mentioned above, are undoubtedly significant. What strikes me as being no less so is the absolute editorial silence which even so liberal a paper as the *Journal de Genève* observed on suggestions made in an uncommonly long article published in its brief and rare pages.

The fact appears to have been that, in 1831, Swiss public opinion was not yet prepared seriously to consider such a revolution as the adoption of the American federal system would have implied.[75] For most of its friends in Switzerland, the introduction of that system still appeared as a distant and an almost Utopian ideal and one to which it was unwise openly to commit oneself for fear of arousing popular antagonism against all forms of centralization. For its conservative opponents, on the other hand, it served as a convenient tool for that very purpose and as a formidable weapon to combat all progress. To accuse even the most cautious reformer of being at heart favorable to anything as incompatible with cantonal sovereignty as the American system was at once to array against him and his proposals a host of popular prejudices. Hence the generally observed reticence.

In order fully to explain the state of the public mind in Switzerland at this moment on the subject of a reform of

[75] The petitions received by the federal authorities, in 1831 and 1832, although sometimes expressing the hope that the Swiss confederation of states would be transformed into a federal state, contained no reference either to the United States, or to the bicameral system. Cf. Archives fédérales, *Beilagen zum Protokoll der Revision-Kommission* (1832).

the Pact of 1815, it may be useful to submit the following considerations:

The forces and influences which were operative in favor of the reform were essentially threefold:

First, the generally felt dissatisfaction with the existing régime, under which the federal authorities had been unable to defend the dignity and the security of the country abroad and to protect the established constitutional order within the cantons.

Second, the ambitions of most of the leaders of the local revolutions. These revolutions had secured the triumph of the principles of freedom and equality and had overthrown the rule of the privileged families in all the largest and in most of the wealthiest cantons. Their leaders, therefore, naturally wished to extend these conquests to the Confederation as a whole. This wish was both political and ideological. It was political or defensive, in that it sprang from a desire to consolidate their achievements at home by protecting them by federal action against any possible reactions from within and from without. And it was aggressively ideological in that it was inspired by a crusading urge to combat everywhere the aristocratic and clerical influences which had been overcome at home and thus to secure for all the benefits of a philosophy which had been reaped by part of the Swiss people only.

Third and finally, economic pressure. The impediments to intercantonal trade and to Swiss industry generally, resulting from the diversity of local currencies and of the prevailing system of weights and measures, from the levy of internal tolls and customs and from the lack of guaranteed freedom of establishment of Swiss citizens in cantons other than their own, all contributed to strengthen the desire for more national unity.

Now, as long as the Diet remained as it was and retained the sole and supreme authority in the Confederation, all progress seemed impossible. No action could be expected of a body of plenipotentiaries whose decisions in all important matters could be carried out only if unanimous and if ratified by the approval of all the cantons.

The obstacles blocking the road to more centralization were formidable, however. If all Swiss, for one reason or another—and these reasons were sometimes contradictory—desired a

stronger federal state, very few were prepared to pay the necessary price. The absolute sovereignty of their own individual
cantons, which of course could not be respected if a more
perfect union was to be effected, was quite as dear to most of
the would-be reformers of the federal constitution as it was
to their opponents.

To the latter it was obviously all the more sacred as the
reformers made no secret of their general ambitions. The
clerical, the aristocratic and the traditional conservative parties
were resolutely determined to maintain their local rights precisely for the reasons which made the anti-clerical, the democratic and the radical parties anxious to invade them.

Moreover, even the liberal French and Italian-speaking cantons were most reluctant to sacrifice, on the altar of national
unity and of their own political philosophy, the local autonomy
which alone protected them against the predominance of the
German-speaking majority. Now although clericals, aristocrats,
convinced conservatives, French- and Italian-speaking citizens
were, and still are, all minorities in Switzerland, combined
together they did, and still do, constitute a popular majority.

Finally, even in the German-speaking Protestant and liberal
cantons, the progressive leaders whom the democratic revolutions had brought to the fore were not all equally impatient to
surrender part of the independence of the cantons, over which
their newly won rule was supreme, to a stronger Confederation,
in which their influence might be more limited.

Thus, although in theory the Swiss people may, on the
whole, be taken to have favored a federal constitutional reform
in the thirties of the last century, in practice even the will
to effect it was uncertain. And if the will was uncertain, the
way was blocked by reasons of technical procedure.

The Pact of 1815, which was to be revised, contained no
clause relating to its revision. According to the prevailing
opinion, it could, therefore, be legally revised only by the
unanimous consent of the signatory cantons. Hence, short of a
revolution, there was no way of modifying its essential terms
in the face of the existing opposition. This was soon to become
manifest alike to the friends of radical reform along American
lines, who were bent on stirring up public opinion in its
favor, and to the more moderate revisionists, who sought to

achieve their purposes by negotiations at the Diet. Let us now briefly consider the efforts of the latter.

The above-mentioned proposal made by Thurgau on May 25, 1831, that the Diet be invited to consider the revision of the Pact of 1815, was submitted to that body on August 19, 1831. The reception it received on the part of the majority of the cantons was decidedly frigid. Only nine, that is, less than a majority, were in favor of its immediate examination. Three more, constituting a bare majority of twelve, were prepared to have it referred to the next meeting of the Diet. Of the ten remaining cantons, some were absolutely opposed even to the discussion of any constitutional amendment whatever. The others, while admitting that the Pact might call for some improvement, declared that the times were not propitious for the consideration of the question.[76]

The composition of these various groups was significant. The most impatient were all cantons that had recently undergone democratic revolutions and that looked upon a revision of the Federal Pact as a necessary corollary thereto. The most conservative were the small, strictly Catholic cantons. The latter both most loathed the revolutionary, anti-clerical spirit of the former and most feared any federal centralization which, encroaching upon their cantonal sovereignty, would expose their populations to the dangers of liberal contamination. Between the two was a group of moderately liberal cantons, which admitted the need for constitutional reform, but repudiated the idea that it should be undertaken by means of a constituent assembly and that it should lead to any constitutional recognition of the inequality of the cantons.

None of the views expressed in this first debate, not even those of Zurich and Saint-Gall, who with Thurgau took the lead among the reformers, could be said to be very bold. They did not go beyond the reëstablishment of that measure of federal centralization which had prevailed under the Act of Mediation. No one even suggested the possibility of setting up a federal parliament. The preference shown by Zurich and endorsed by Saint-Gall for a double representation of the larger

[76] *Abschied der eidgenössischen Tagsatzung 1831*, pp. 71 *et seq.*; *Mémorial des séances du Conseil représentatif*, 4e année (Genève, 1831-1832), pp. 531 *et seq.*; W. E. Rappard, *L'individu et l'Etat dans l'évolution constitutionnelle de la Suisse* (Zurich, 1936), pp. 222 *et seq.*

cantons in the Diet called for an immediate protest on the part of several of the smaller ones. Even Schaffhausen, which was otherwise among the more progressive, would not hear of it.

The official record of the meeting contains no mention whatever of the United States. But as the statements made in the Diet were rarely reported *in extenso*, that does not prove that no such mention was made. In his account of the meeting, Baumgartner, who had attended it as delegate of Saint-Gall, says that Oertli, the delegate from Appenzell, who was listed among the most ardent friends of reform, declared that, "very desirable as the strengthening of the Confederation was, the Swiss people were not ripe for arrangements such as were suggested by the model of the North American free state. They were all too deeply attached to their old federalism for that."[77]

The first official encounter between the advocates and the opponents of a revision of the Federal Pact was of course in no way decisive. It was only in the nature of a preliminary skirmish, but its results did show the general desires and the relative force of the conflicting parties. The majority of the cantons and—since this included all the larger ones—an even greater majority of the Swiss people, were in favor of reform. But even this majority, and, of course, still more the small but resolute minority that was opposed to all change, were as yet very firmly attached to the principle of cantonal sovereignty. This was still generally looked upon as the cornerstone of the Swiss Confederation.

When, on July 16, 1832, the Diet came to consider the question which had been referred to it by its predecessor, the prospects were somewhat more favorable for the friends of reform. Already a few months before, the official delegates of the seven leading cantons, which had recently undergone a democratic revolution, had met semi-privately and secretly to draft a treaty of mutual guarantee by which their cantons, which promptly ratified it, undertook to protect each others' constitutions. Although the treaty was later opened to the signature of all other cantons which wished to adhere to it, and although it was then communicated to the Diet, such a special arrangement distinctly implied a lack of confidence in the Confederation as a whole and especially in its Pact. It was but logical, therefore,

[77] Baumgartner, *op. cit.*, vol. I, p. 178.

that its authors should at the same time adopt a common line of action in the matter of constitutional reform.

They did so by framing and publishing a revised-draft federal constitution.[78] Their plan, somewhat on the lines of the Act of Mediation, provided for a unicameral Diet in which the cantons would enjoy representation graded roughly according to their population. Although this plan was published anonymously and privately, its authors, of whom Casimir Pfyffer and Baumgartner were the most active, were immediately suspected of being the same influential liberal statesmen who had negotiated the treaty of mutual guarantee.

Their ideas were therefore discussed in all the leading papers. It is interesting, especially for our purpose, to note the following comment they drew from the pen of Pellegrino Rossi, who was shortly to play an important part in the debates at the Diet. In a paper he had recently founded mainly to discuss Swiss federal affairs, this publicist from Geneva wrote, immediately upon receiving a copy of the project:

It tends to transform the confederation of states into a true federal state, up to a certain point resembling that of North America . . . One may ask if such a change is possible or in any case easy in a country which for five to six - centuries has lived under the present system. Are the historical antecedents the same as those of the United States of America? . . . These questions deserve to be examined even by those who, like ourselves, are inclined to admit that, abstractly considered, the American system is distinctly superior to the Swiss one.[79]

The federal Diet resumed its consideration of the problem of revision on July 16, 1832. As the meeting had been preceded not only by much public discussion but also by repeated private exchanges of views between the various delegations, its debates were far less rambling and more definite than those of the preceding year. But they revealed the existence of the same three general tendencies. The first and the most progressive was that of the seven cantons who had formed an inner league among themselves. Its spokesmen advocated amendments similar to those above-mentioned in their private project, but still appreciably less radical. This tendency was combated by

[78] *Entwurf einer schweizerischen Bundesverfassung.* Von einer Gesellschaft Eidgenossen (Zurich, 1832).
[79] *Le Fédéral,* April 10, 1832.

the conservative Catholic cantons, which practically opposed any change. Between these two groups was a third, counting six cantons and the Protestant half-canton of Appenzell Ausser Rhoden, which were favorable to a strengthening of the federal bond, but would not hear of any unequal representation in the Diet.

On July 17, 1832, a majority, thirteen and a half cantons, formally resolved "that the Federal Pact of the XXII cantons of Switzerland of August 7, 1815, be subjected to a revision" and that a committee of fifteen delegates be entrusted with the task of preparing a revised draft.[80]

This draft was promptly elaborated. Known as the Rossi Pact, by the name of its rapporteur, the delegate from Geneva, it was published with the latter's report as a state document at the end of the year.[81]

Without attempting to analyze the 120 articles of this draft and to sum up the 119 pages of the accompanying commentary, I shall merely seek to characterize the scheme as a whole and to quote a few lines from the report.

The scheme as a whole was very obviously the result of a compromise between the first and the third of the above-mentioned parties, a compromise in which the first conceded more than it gained. It is built up on the principle of cantonal sovereignty and, accordingly, maintains equal representation in the Diet. The fact that the document was called an "act," and neither a pact nor a constitution, was in itself significant. The progressives had objected to the retention of the term "pact," as implying the maintenance of the existing régime, and the moderates to the adoption of the term "constitution," as indicating the substitution of national for cantonal sovereignty. In spite of its timidity, however, the draft scheme would, if adopted, have in fact transformed Switzerland into a federal state, in some ways more, and in others less, unified than Switzerland had been under the Act of Mediation.

In his very eloquent report, which still makes excellent reading today, Rossi defines as follows the main idea underlying the draft:

[80] *Abschied* 1832, pp. 115 *et seq.*; Baumgartner, *op. cit.*, vol. I, pp. 332 *et seq.*
[81] *Projet d'Acte fédéral et rapport de la commission de la Diète aux XXII cantons suisses* (Geneva, December 1832).

The sovereignty of the cantons in Switzerland is the historical and fundamental principle, the expression of the past and of the present. But this principle, this expression, is today more than ever qualified by another idea, the idea of the common fatherland, of a general interest which must be consolidated and protected.[82]

Although the "Project of Federal Act" is not very unlike the draft which Rossi had, a few months before, in his paper, likened to the constitution of the United States, his report contained but one reference to American conditions. When setting forth the reason which had led the committee to retain the principle of equal representation in the Diet, he wrote:

The United States of America have adopted unequal representation. The effect is more apparent than real. Besides the suspensive presidential veto, the United States have two houses, whose agreement is necessary for the enactment of laws. As in the Senate each state is represented by two members, there is no inequality.

It would be impossible in Switzerland to introduce the system of two houses of legislature—to say nothing of the presidential veto. One could not expect the cantons to pay for the services of a large number of deputies nor the federal treasury to assume the enormous expense of their subsistence.[83]

It is, I am afraid, rather characteristic of my country that such an important possibility should have been dismissed for such a paltry consideration. As a matter of fact, it was not only nor even mainly the instinct of economy, but the still stronger instincts of habit and of tradition that had to be overcome in Switzerland before the bicameral system could be adopted, as. it finally was sixteen years later.

In spite of the care and the caution with which it had been drafted, the proposed act was not to find favor with the federal Diet. It was discussed in the following year and its progressive features were still further whittled down by several amendments.[84]

It was in fact killed by the electorate of Lucerne who, in a popular referendum, on July 6, 1833, had overwhelmingly rejected it. As under the Act of 1832 the city of Lucerne was to have been the federal capital—a great concession made by

[82] *Ibid.*, p. 21.
[83] *Ibid.*, p. 84.
[84] *Abschied*, 1833, a, pp. 20 *et seq.*; 1833, pp. 80 *et seq.*

Berne and Zurich in the hope that it would placate the small Catholic cantons bordering on the Lake of Lucerne—and as the canton of Lucerne, the home of Casimir Pfyffer, had heretofore always voted with the progressive group, the negative popular verdict was generally looked upon as decisive. Rossi, who heard of it in Paris, where he was soon to take up his residence, to become a French citizen, member of the French House of Peers and professor at the Collège de France, before becoming Ambassador to Rome and then Minister of the Pope, wrote to a friend in Geneva:

> The decision of Lucerne has produced a great impression here. One wonders what will become of Switzerland if, as may be feared, the example is followed by others, and if, on the other hand, the radical party, refusing to return to the Pact of 1815, attempts to carry out its plan of a federal constituent assembly.[85]

The drafts of 1832 and 1833 were unsuccessful compromises. Not only could they arouse no enthusiasm—compromises seldom do—but they failed in their main purpose, which was at least to moderate the hostility of their foes.

These were to be found principally, but not exclusively, on the right. The extreme liberals and the radicals on the left also rejected the compromises. Thus Casimir Pfyffer voted against the draft of 1833 in the Grand Council at Lucerne. In clear, although moderate, terms he explained that he could not honestly favor a scheme which would allow twelve small cantons —the conservative Catholic cantons were the least populous— to lay down the law and impose their will on the rest of the country. That might very well imply that one quarter of the population of Switzerland would rule over the other three quarters and thus endanger the latter's democratic conquests. That state of affairs, which had been barely tolerable under the pact of 1815—which was in the nature of an international treaty between sovereign cantons—was entirely intolerable in the constitution of what was to have been a federal state.[86]

It is interesting to note, in view of the coming evolution towards the American bicameral system, that it was thus the

[85] Cf. Gustave Dolt, *Lettres politiques de Pellegrino Rossi au Syndic J. J. Rigaud, 1832-1841* (Geneva, 1932), p. 113.

[86] Dr. Kasimir Pfyffer, *Geschichte des Kantons Luzern, op. cit.*, vol. II, pp. 487 *et seq.*

question of the legislature which prevented one of the most distinguished of the liberal leaders to vote for the compromise.

THE STRUGGLE FOR AND AGAINST THE "AMERICAN SYSTEM," 1833-1847

With the failure of constitutional reform in 1833, there begins a long period of struggle for and against the adoption of the so-called "American system."

While the opposition of Casimir Pfyffer to the draft of 1833 had been moderate and discreet, that of the radical extremists on the contrary was violent and most vociferous. Chief among these was Pfyffer's fellow-citizen from Beromünster, in Lucerne, the doctor philosopher Ignaz Paul Vital Troxler.[87] As Troxler was, perhaps more than any other single person, responsible for the adoption of the American bicameral system in Switzerland, he deserves a special mention here.

Born in 1780 as the son of modest, devout (but not superstitious) Catholic parents, he soon distinguished himself in his studies. In 1798 he at first welcomed the Helvetic Republic and the principles of liberty and equality which it proclaimed. Very soon, however, disappointment replaced enthusiasm. Having been appointed to a government position in Lucerne at the age of eighteen, he became disgusted with the general disorder which he witnessed and with the predominance of French influence in Swiss affairs. In 1800 he left his position and his country to study medicine and philosophy at Jena and later at Göttingen. He returned to his native Beromünster at the age of twenty-six. From then on he lived in Switzerland: first practicing medicine at Beromünster, and then teaching—at Lucerne from 1819 to 1823, at Aarau from 1823 to 1830, at Basle in 1830-1831, then again in Aarau from 1831 to 1834 and finally in Berne from 1834 to 1853. He died in 1866.

Thus his active existence, as also his political views, were far more Swiss than cantonal, in contrast to the existence and the views of most of his fellow-countrymen. Throughout his long and varied career he read and wrote philosophy, sought

---

[87] A. Götz, *Dr. Ignaz Paul Vital Troxler* (Zurich, 1915); Charles Secretan, *Troxler*, in *Biographies Nationales* (Lausanne, 1883), vol. III, pp. 111-128; Cf. also some interesting impressions of a foreign contemporary in T. Mundt, *Spaziergänge und Weltfahrten* (Altona, 1839), vol. III, pp. 40 *et seq.*

rather than shunned—it would seem—controversy and law-
suits, attacked the governments of the day, and published
countless pamphlets which were more often violently polemic
than serenely enlightening.

The political philosophy which he expounded with real con-
sistency through all his life was that of a rabid anti-aristocrat
and anti-traditionalist more than of a thoroughgoing democratic radical. He was too much attached to culture, and also
to a free type of religion, not to be antagonized by certain
demagogic manifestations of the leaders of the politically-
emancipated masses. But he was, above all, opposed to unjus-
tified hereditary privilege and to irrational routine in all its
forms. From 1813 on he published one or more books and
pamphlets every year, dealing successively with matters philosophical, medical, pedagogical and political. During the Restoration, he was naturally always in opposition to the cantonal
and the federal régime of his country. His presidential address
at the meeting of the Helvetic Society, in 1822, was a protest
against governmental repression and a plea for popular liberty
and national unity. After 1830, he interested himself principally in constitutional federal reform.

The draft of 1832 was hardly out of the hands of the printers
when Troxler showered down upon it a hailstorm of denunci-
atory pamphlets. Strangely disguising his real historical erudi-
tion and original philosophical thought behind a barrage of
violent invective, he flayed the projected federal act, laid bare
its "seven capital sins" and repudiated it utterly as the "bastard" product of a "quasi-legitimist doctrine." It would lead
us too far afield to analyze or even to summarize all these
pamphlets,[88] of which no less than eight appeared in 1833 alone.

[88] *Über Verderbnis und Herstellung der Eidgenossenschaft; in Reden.* (Severus
Pertinax, Rapperswil, 1832); *Über die von einem Tagsatzungsausschuss des
Jahres 1832 entworfene Bundesurkunde* (1833); *Die sieben Todsünden der
Bundesurkunde* (1833); *Die eine und wahre Eidgenossenschaft im Gegensatz zur
Zentralherrschaft und Kantonstümelei, sowie zum neuen Zwitterbunde beider;
nebst einem Verfassungsentwurf* (Rapperswil, 1833); *Maibüchlein für das
Schweizervolk.* (Novalis, Stäfa, 1833); *Der von der Tagsatzung am Recht der
Nation begangene Verrat grundsätzlich nachgewiesen.* (Pertinax Novalis, Stäfa
(?), 1833); *Reden, gehalten in der aargauischen Grossratssitzung am 23. und
25. Juli 1833* von Troxler, Hürner, Tanner, etc., den Entwurf der neuen
Bundesurkunde betreffend (1833); *Lösung der nationalen Lebensfrage. Worauf
muss die Bundesverfassung der Eidgenossenschaft begründet werden?* (Rapperswil, 1833).

Rather would I quote from one of them[89] a passage which may be taken to have laid the foundations of the bridge over which the American constitutional idea was imported into Switzerland. Having therein recalled the past constitutional evolution of his country, he wrote:

This undeniable development leads us to the conclusion that the true equilibrium to which it tends can be found neither in a confederation of states nor in a unitary state, and that an "Eidgenossenschaft"[90] can only be a federal state,—indeed, is nothing but its most perfect form . . . The unitary state excludes the constituent states from the league and the confederation excludes its citizens . . . The federal state alone reconciles two apparently contradictory principles and satisfies alike two opposite sets of claims . . .

We have to harmonize together a qualitative and a quantitative relation or rather to reconcile the representation of two so-called principles of nature and of ideals in the constitution of the supreme authority of our federal state. For the twofold exigency of freedom within and independence without demands that both cantonal diversities and national unity find their representation and their guarantee in our league.

In the course of my long and earnest reflections on the problem, a brilliant and happy example of its solution in historical reality loomed up before my eyes. It was the federal system of North America. The federal assembly of the United States (the Congress) is divided into two branches, into the Council of the Elders (the Senate) and in that of the deputies (House of Representatives). The first is elected and composed by the legislatures of the constituent states . . . the second, on the other hand, by the people on the basis of population . . .

The constitution of the United States of America is a great work of art which the human mind created according to the eternal laws of its divine nature. It is the product of the united new culture of mankind. It is a model and a pattern for the organization of the public life of republics in general, in which the whole and the parts shall both be free and equal. In the year 1787 the Convention at Philadelphia solved the great problem of the conciliation of national unity with the autonomy of constituent states and this autonomy with the freedom of all citizens. The problem has been solved by the new world for all peoples, states and countries.

[89] Professor Dr. Troxler, *Die eine und wahre Eidgenossenschaft*, etc., *op. cit.*

[90] The official German name of the Swiss Confederation, which literally translated means "a community by oath."

The civically free and federally united social organization it has created is a response to a natural necessity just as the organic structure of men, of animals and of plants.[91]

To the pamphlet in which this important statement is made Troxler added a "draft fundamental law for the Swiss Confederation," divided into 49 paragraphs.[92] Of these, we quote those which most clearly show both how he was, in framing them, influenced by his American model and how he in turn seems to have influenced the framers of the present Swiss constitution:

§ 1

The Swiss *Eidgenossenschaft* is a federal state based upon the foundation of popular sovereignty with representative institutions.

§ 2

The unity of the whole shall be combined with the autonomy of the parts and accordingly the sovereignty of the nation must be exercised in the league by a general and by a special representation.

§ 3

The general representation in the league is that of the Swiss citizens or companions of oath (Eidgenossen), the special representation that of their states or cantons.

. . . .

§ 34

The sovereign in the federal state is only one, namely, the nation; but the nature of the federal state demands that its representative organization be twofold, namely, the original or general in the free states, or that of the population, and the derivative or special, or that of the cantons in the league.

. . . .

[91] This last passage is drafted in terms so characteristic of the German metaphysics in which Troxler had been trained and in which his mind always seemed to revel that I cannot be certain of my translation. In the original it reads: "Die Aufgabe ist durch die neue Welt gelöst für alle Völker, Staaten und Länder, und die in ihrer Lösung aufgestellte freibürgerliche und bundesgenössische Gesellschaftsgestaltung hat ihre Naturnothwendigkeit, wie der Organismus der Menschen, Thiere und Pflanzen." *Ibid.*, p. 28.

[92] *Entwurf eines Grundgesetzes für die schweizerische Eidgenossenschaft, ibid.*, pp. 31 *et seq.*

§ 36

The representation of the cantons is the fruit of a historical tradition ("ist ein herkömmlich Gegebenes"). As a state in the league, a canton cannot have more or less than one representative . . .

. . . . ̄

§ 38

The representation of the nation rests on the population . . .

§ 39

The national representation is constituted by one representative for every 25,000 inhabitants . . .

. . . .

§ 42

The federal authorities are constituted by a legislature, an executive council and a supreme court.

§ 43

The legislature, or national congress, is divided into two branches, an assembly of representatives of the people and an assembly of representatives of the cantons . . .

§ 44

A federal chief ("Bundesammann") with two deputies constitutes the executive council. All three are to be elected at a meeting of both councils sitting together as a diet. They may be freely chosen from the body of the citizens, but during their tenure of office they may be members neither of the council of senators nor of the council of representatives.

To the conception thus outlined Troxler remained faithful throughout his life. Fifteen years later, on the morrow of the Swiss civil war which finally broke down the resistance of the opponents and made possible the adoption of a truly federal constitution, he published one of his last political pamphlets under the title "The constitution of the United States of America as a model for the Swiss federal reform."[93]

As a preface to the translation of the American constitution,

[93] *Die Verfassung der Vereinigten Staaten Nordamerika's als Musterbild der Schweizerischen Bundesreform* (Schaffhausen, 1848).

he renewed the profession of his political faith in almost the
same terms as those of 1833, writing:

A rich experience of life made up of much suffering, great sacri-
fices and varied struggles led the author to political studies and
bred in him the conviction *that the authors of the fundamental
law of the United States of America have solved a truly human
problem. Through their federal constitution they have translated
into life an ideal of social organization which from now on in
the history of the world must be looked upon as the authoritative
pattern of all federal republics.*[94]

It is impossible to determine with accuracy what positive influence Troxler himself exerted on the course of events in
Switzerland between the dates of publication of the two pamphlets we have singled out from among a host of other of his
writings. Two things, however, are certain. On the one hand,
his ideas were taken up, reported and elaborated by a small
group of ardent reformers, among whom he expressly mentioned, in 1848, Kasthofer, James Fazy and Druey.[95] On the
other hand, although they were widely known and discussed
throughout the country in the interval, they were rarely if ever
mentioned in the official constitutional debates of the Diet.
The natural reluctance of professional politicians to admit
their intellectual debts to academic outsiders and also the fear
of exasperating the opposition of the impenitent believers in
cantonal sovereignty are probably responsible for this otherwise surprising reticence. Before noting how the pressure of
events finally forced the American solution upon Swiss official-
dom in 1848, let us briefly recall how, following in Troxler's
footsteps, a few other Swiss publicists sought to popularize his
ideals.

One of the most effective of these was the Bernese government forester Karl Kasthofer. That he was a forester by taste,
as well as by calling, is shown by the fact that most of his
publications deal with the subject of forestry. It is all the more
remarkable that, after taking an active but not a leading part
in the cantonal revolution at Berne, he should at the age of 55
have found time to study the American constitution and felt
called upon to urge his compatriots to reconstruct their country according to its principles. This he did most convincingly

[94] In italics in the original text. *Ibid.*, p. 11.
[95] *Ibid.*, p. 12.

in a pamphlet entitled "The Swiss Federal Booklet."[96] It appeared in 1833 at Burgdorf, a country town in the Canton of Berne which had been one of the centers of the cantonal revolution. To this popularly written pamphlet, he annexed a translation of the greater part of the American constitution of 1787. In his introduction he expressly and sympathetically referred to Troxler's efforts, which shows that he was deliberately following the latter's lead.

For the purposes of this study, the whole booklet would deserve quoting. No publication more clearly shows the reasons and the nature of the interest the enlightened and unprejudiced Swiss of a century ago took in the American precedent. That interest was one of principle as well as of political technique. It was one of principle and of instinctive attraction, as the Americans, in Kasthofer's eyes, were like his fellow-countrymen—freedom-loving republicans who had revolted against foreign rule in order to be their own masters. And it was one of constitutional technique also, since the problem with which they were confronted on the morrow of their war of independence was essentially the same as that which was baffling the members of the Swiss federal Diet. How could local liberty and local diversities be respected without jeopardizing national unity? It was to that difficult problem that the Americans had found a technically felicitous solution.

The following passage I have selected for quotation because it brings out these two points. It is interesting also in that it shows that the advocacy of what came currently to be called "the American system" had already gone far enough to arouse the national prejudice against everything foreign, which is characteristic of the Swiss, as of most other democracies. Kasthofer wrote:

The wonderful prosperity of North America has attracted millions of emigrants from all European countries, including thousands from Switzerland alone. The contentment and the welfare which they have found abroad are such as to make desirable for all of you, my friends, an acquaintance with the constitution which has brought with it such blessings and which teaches all of us Swiss a most significant and useful lesson. Don't tell me what our old

[96] Karl Kasthofer, *Das Schweizerische Bundesbüchli* (Burgdorf, 1833). Cf. also by the same: *Mein politisches Glaubensbekenntnis am Schlusse des Jahres 1834* (Berne, 1835), in which he refers to his relations with Troxler and Bornhauser, p. XIII.

politicians have told us for centuries past and what our new-baked grand masters are repeating today: that we should and can learn nothing from an example which cannot be adequate and helpful for us because we Swiss are a very special people, because our country is entirely different from other countries and because our conditions are such that they cannot be organized and moulded according to a foreign pattern. Men and their passions are everywhere about alike and their needs, their sufferings, their satisfactions, their force and their happiness all spring from very similar sources. Let us learn from the example of other peoples: a people that refuses to learn anything cannot escape dangerous accidents, nay even its destruction.

The North Americans . . . after their ten years' struggle against the English . . . nobility and against the king . . . were in a position similar to ours: they also had their special states or cantons which did not wish to sacrifice their independence, their customs, their particular administration; some of these cantons were peopled by Scotch, English and Irish; others by French, others by Spaniards, others finally mostly by Germans; some were Catholic, others followed the Reformed, others the Lutheran faith; some were liberals and republicans, the others royalists; some lived in hot, others in cold, climates; some in rolling country, some in lowlands, others in high mountains; some were and are engaged in large trades and in manufactures in great sea ports, others, many hundred hours travel from the coast, live only on agriculture and cattle-raising; there you find a hundred thousand black Africans in the employ of white planters, here nothing but free white farmers; here half-savage Indian hunters are welcomed into the social fold, there none of these natives are any more to be found.

And all these so diverse peoples scattered over this immeasurably large land are united into one "Eidgenossenschaft," without losing their freedom; all these cantons situated thousands of miles from each other, separated by high mountains, by the greatest rivers in the world, by religion, by speech, habits and old customs, are bound together without loss of independence and impaired possibilities of development by a federal bond which gives them the might of the greatest powers of the world and secures their freedom against any foe.[97]

Having thus sought to refute what even then was already the main argument of the opponents of the American system in Switzerland, namely, the greater complexity of conditions at

[97] *Ibid.*, p. 12 *et seq.*

home, Kasthofer went on to expound the pure federal and bicameral doctrine by analyzing and favorably commenting on the main provisions of the American constitution. In the light of these considerations, he then formulated "The main principles of a new Swiss league" which were but the American principles of 1787 adapted to his country. The Congress was called Diet, the House of Representatives, National Assembly and the Senate, Senate.[98]

In language both less learned and less passionately violent than Troxler, the elderly Bernese forester Kasthofer preached precisely the same political philosophy as the physician philosopher from Lucerne.

The only other German-Swiss popular propagandist of American constitutionalism in the early thirties of the last century whom I shall mention here was Thomas Bornhauser, the political pastor from Thurgau. After actively promoting the cantonal revolution at home in 1830 by his fiery oratory, as we have seen above, he, in 1833, joined with Troxler and Kasthofer in a common effort to win over the whole Swiss people to American federalism and bicameralism with his pen.[99] His literary contribution resembled neither the passionate and erudite pamphlets of Troxler, nor the popularly didactic booklet of Kasthofer. He delivered his sermon in the form of a dialogue. The principal characters were ordinary Swiss citizens of divergent political views, such as one could meet on the market place of any small town. The scene is laid at Arbon in Thurgau on the Lake of Constance where Bornhauser resided. There is no plot, but the political problems of the day are discussed from various angles. The leading character, Treuherz, who is the author's spokesman, advocates the American system as a guide for constitutional reform.[100]

· The question is broached as a group of German emigrants coming over the lake appear on the stage. In reply to a question as to their plans, one of these emigrants says:[101]

---

[98] *Ibid.*, p. 19 *et seq.*

[99] On May 21, 1832 he had already delivered a public lecture on the reform of the federal constitution, but without referring to the American precedent. Cf. T. Bornhauser, *Ein Wort über die Revision der schweizerischen Bundesakte,* Trogen, 1832.

[100] *Schweizerbart und Treuherz,* Saint-Gall, 1834.

[101] I quote from the French translation, *Schweizerbart et Treuherz,* transl. (Leresche, 1835), pp. 59 *et seq.*

The night of slavery surrounded our cradle, the sun of liberty shall shine upon our grave; we are bound for the country of Washington.

To Treuherz, who suggests that Switzerland also is a free country, the emigrant replies:

Switzerland is weak because it is the prey of dissension . . . let us leave for the country of Washington where happiness born of freedom is wedded to power, the child of concord.

After the departure of these grandiloquent German emigrants, the conversation between the Swiss who remain continues as follows:

The school master: "Why should everybody wish to go to North America?"

The alderman: "There are lots of vacant lands there. That is what attracts the emigrants."

Treuherz: "It is also, and perhaps more still, the greater religious, political and civil freedom."

The school master: "What I don't understand is why Germans should not prefer to settle in Switzerland and why even Swiss should think of leaving for America."

The alderman: "Everything seems more attractive from afar."

Treuherz: "I agree with that remark . . . but we must admit as true what is true. In fact, North America has advantages of which Switzerland is still deprived."

The school master: "What are they?" . . .

Treuherz: ". . . Our ancient and vicious federal institutions have so demoralized us that many Swiss cannot even imagine a different and happier state; that is why the men who propose a complete reconstruction of our institutions are denounced as dangerous innovators, as dreamers and as madmen. Even our alderman here seems to look upon a federal state in which the cantonal and the national spheres would be harmonized one with another as a Utopian ideal. Well, the problem has been solved. The United States of North America have founded a federal state in which the freedom of each individual canton stands in perfect harmony with the unity of the nation."

The alderman: "I am not sufficiently informed about the federal constitution of North America."

Treuherz: "In that country a careful distinction is made between what belongs to the confederation and what concerns the individual states or cantons. War and peace, treaties and foreign alliances, provisions relating to the acquisition of citizenship, the currency, weights and measures, the postal service, the customs and the army are all federal affairs which are dealt with by Congress (the Diet). This Congress is made up of two authorities or Chambers. The House of Representatives and the Senate. The House of Representatives is the organ of the nation, the Senate that of the cantons."

The alderman: "Thus the United States have a system of two houses which seems to recall the constitution of England?"

Treuherz: "The representatives are elected in proportion to the population, one for every 33,000 inhabitants. Thus, for instance, New Hampshire sends three representatives to. the House, Massachusetts, eight; New York, six; New Jersey, four; Connecticut, five; Virginia, ten; Delaware, one."

Schweizerbart: "That seems reasonable. The canton that is most inhabited and that contributes most to federal expenditure should also have most representatives."

Treuherz: "Still the Senate is annexed to the House of Representatives so that the interests of the canton should not be neglected. Here population is not taken into account: every canton, be it large or small, sends two deputies to the Senate."

The alderman: "How about their instructions?"

Treuherz: "That absurd institution is absolutely unknown in the United States. The members of the House of Representatives as also those of the Senate vote freely according to their conviction. However, in order to avoid light-hearted decisions, every bill is submitted to a triple examination. That is to say that, before being enacted, it must be adopted by the House of Representatives and by the Senate and approved by the President. The latter is the supreme executive official of the Confederation and has the army under his orders."

The alderman: "If the members of the House and the Senate vote without instructions, I don't understand how the Senate can represent the interests of the canton?"

Treuherz: "There is, however, a certain counterpoise in that, whereas the House of Representatives is elected according to population, each canton has the same number of deputies in the Senate; but this counterpoise is light because the senators do not necessarily subordinate the federal to the cantonal interests. As many of us at first, Franklin also was opposed to this system of two houses, in which he saw an imitation of the British constitution. Now several of our distinguished fellow-citizens have proposed that we adopt this system. It seems to me that the principal merit of the constitution of the United States resides in this: that a clear distinction is made between what are federal and what are cantonal affairs, that the former are unreservedly entrusted to a large national body which considers them freely, whereas the second are dealt with by the legislature of the cantons. Thereby one avoids on the one hand the disunion from which we Swiss are suffering at present and on the other, the error committed by the Helvetic government when it wished to govern the whole of Switzerland from Berne, as if it were a monarchy."

Schweizerbart: "The President seems to be a very powerful man in the United States; I should think almost too powerful for us in Switzerland."

Treuherz: "That is why he is elected, he and the vice-president, by the whole nation and only for a term of four years. We Swiss should never forget that the legislative authorities should be as numerous as possible and the executive authorities, on the contrary, as few as possible."

The school master: "Have the Americans of the United States also a supreme federal tribunal?"

Treuherz: "Yes."

Schweizerbart: "Does the Congress sit permanently?"

Treuherz: "It meets as a rule only once a year in the month of December."

Schweizerbart: "If that is so, the federal constitution of the United States must not be very costly to run."

Treuherz: "The Americans are free and happy under that constitution. The greatness, the power and the wealth of their Confederation are increasing from year to year. As one readily understands, not all American institutions can be copied in Switzerland; we should, however, base our new federal constitution on the fundamental principles which experience has so gloriously consecrated beyond the Atlantic; then the happiness born of freedom would with us also be wedded to power, the child of concord."

Schweizerbart: "If the citizens of the United States of North America have such a good consitution that hundreds, that thousands of peoples should annually be leaving their own country and undertaking such a long voyage in order to live and to die under its rule, what is there to prevent us from introducing this constitution immediately in its essential elements? It depends only on us; a people can aspire to no more than to be the arbiter of its own destinies."

It is not difficult to understand that this vivid and popular discussion of the American constitution should have been sold in several editions and very widely read all over Switzerland.

Troxler, Kasthofer, and Bornhauser were all German-Swiss. They were born and bred in the German part of Switzerland.

They had studied at German-speaking universities—Troxler and Kasthofer in Germany, Bornhauser at Zurich. None of them had ever enjoyed any close association with France and with French thought.

Druey and Fazy, the two other most prominent popular advocates of the American system in Switzerland in the thirties of the last century were, on the contrary, pure French-Swiss. Both of them, it is true, had also spent several years in Germany for purpose of study and spoke German,—and English as well, be it incidentally observed. But they had both been born in French-speaking communities—Fazy in Geneva and Druey in a country-town in Vaud—and they both came to be the leading political spokesmen for their native cantons.

Of the two, Henri Druey was the more prominent in federal politics, but the less constantly orthodox in his defense of American bicameral federalism. In 1832, and again in 1840, 1841, 1845, 1846 and 1847, he represented his canton at the Diet. After taking a very active and influential part in the drafting of the federal constitution of 1848, he became a member of the first Federal Council, as the new Swiss executive was called.

In the matter of constitutional reform, he was from the start among the most ardent partisans of centralization. He opposed the Pact Rossi in 1833 not, as the majority of his fellow-Vaudois, because it threatened the sovereignty of the cantons, but on the contrary because it failed to establish the predominance of the federal state.[102] He then joined hands with the German-Swiss radicals who professed similar but not identical views. On February 26, 1834, with Troxler, Kasthofer, Bornhauser and a few others, he became a member of a committee appointed by the Federal Security Society to outline a revised federal constitution.[103] During that year he published a series of articles in the *"Nouvelliste vaudois"* in which he urged the adoption by a federal constituent assembly of a constitution based on the principles of popular sovereignty. The Swiss nation represented in a single diet, composed of members elected by the cantons according to their population, should secure to all of its citizens everywhere the respect of certain fundamental rights.

[102] Leresche, *Henri Druey, op. cit.*, p. 316.
[103] *Ibid.*, p. 318; *Journal de Genève*, March 1, 1834, p. 3.

On all these points, except on that of the federal legislature, Druey was in accord with his German-Swiss associates. But although in one of his articles, he spoke of "the United States of America whose constitution we propose as a model for Switzerland,"[104] he was never enamored of the bicameral system. As a member of the Diet which in 1848 framed the revised federal constitution, he opposed the introduction of that system as long as he could.[105] While almost reluctantly recommending the draft to his fellow citizens in Lausanne after its adoption by the committee, he declared that he felt no "paternal love" for what he looked upon as a rather lame compromise.

Quite different was the attitude of James Fazy of Geneva. Druey, as most of his fellow-constituents, was driven to submit to the bicameral system as the only means of overcoming, or at least, of moderating the opposition of the federalists. Fazy, on the contrary, looked upon it as the most valuable feature of the American constitution. When in political control in Geneva, in 1847, he expressly instructed the Geneva delegation to the Diet to vote in favor of it.

Born in Geneva, in 1794, of an old local family of French Huguenot stock, this strangely brilliant and demagogic founder of modern democracy in his native canton had spent most of his youth in France.[106] In the early twenties of the last century, he had there become intimately acquainted with General La Fayette who aroused in him a deep and lasting enthusiasm for the United States and its institutions. As Fazy wrote in his autobiographical notes, quoted by his kinsman and biographer Henri Fazy:

I shall ever remember all that the General was good enough to explain to me about American institutions during our return one evening alone together in his carriage from his château de la Grange to Paris. It was a complete course of lectures on the subject. If a stenographer had been present to take down what the General told me, the work which M. de Tocqueville published later would have been useless.[107]

From this early time on, we are assured that Fazy was con-

[104] Annex to Leresche, *Ibid.*, p. 11.

[105] Cf. manuscript notes of Jonas Furrer, *Archives fédérales*, 17 a, p. 101.

[106] Henri Fazy, *James Fazy, sa vie et son oeuvre* (Geneva, 1887), p. 1 *et seq.*; H. Barth, *Bibliographie der Schweizer Geschichte*, Vol. I (Basle, 1914), p. 394.

[107] *Ibid.*, p. 17.

vinced that Switzerland would inevitably be led to copy the American federal pattern.[108] Whatever the truth of this suggestion—and it may well be in the nature of retrospective prophecy—one thing is certain:

In September 1831, that is immediately after the first official debate in the Diet, nearly a year before the appointment of the Rossi Committee and nearly two years before the first pamphlets of Troxler, Kasthofer and Bornhauser, there appeared in the *Journal de Genève* an anonymous article whose author asserted that the "federal system of the United States of America" alone fulfilled Switzerland's constitutional needs.[109] What is hardly less certain is the identity of that author. My reasons for recognizing him in James Fazy strike me as absolutely compelling. A few months or years later, there appeared over his signature an undated pamphlet of 32 pages with the following title: "Draft Federal Constitution (articles extracted from the *Journal de Genève*)."[110] In the catalogue of the Geneva Public Library, the probable date of the publication of this pamphlet is given as 1833. Elsewhere, and particularly in Fazy's biography, it has been tentatively dated 1837.[111]

In perusing this pamphlet, I was struck by the familiarity of its contents. On verification, I discovered that the whole of its first chapter, that is 10 out of its 32 pages, was the literal transcription of the *Journal de Genève* article of 1831. The few verbal differences are so slight as to be entirely negligible. Now, either Fazy drafted those pages in 1831 for the *Journal de Genève* or he plagiarized them later. As he was in close touch with the editors of the paper which he had himself founded in 1826, as the views expounded in the article were his at the time, as they were held to be Utopian by almost everybody else and as there is nothing, either in the special circumstances of the case or in the whole subsequent career of Fazy to justify the suspicion of plagiarism, I conclude that the article undoubtedly flowed from his pen.

As for the rest of the pamphlet, which contains a draft federal constitution for Switzerland and allusions to Troxler, Bornhauser and Druey, it does not seem ever to have been pub-

108 Fazy, *op. cit.*, p. 20.
109 Cf. pp. *supra* 50-51.
110 James Fazy, *Projet de constitution fédérale* (Articles extraits du *Journal de Genève*), Geneva.
111 Fazy, *op. cit.*, p. 235.

lished in the *Journal de Genève* at all. As these allusions show, it was obviously written later, probably in 1835. Fragments of the pamphlet are to be found in issues of that year of the *"Europe Centrale,"* which Fazy had founded in December of 1833 as the first daily paper ever to have been published in Geneva.[112] In January and February 1835, Fazy delivered in Geneva a series of public lectures on federal organization. Judging by their syllabus published in the *"Europe Centrale"* these lectures covered appreciably the same ground as the pamphlet and also dealt with a draft federal and bicameral Swiss constitution.[113]

What Fazy thus advocated as a publicist in the early thirties, he very effectively managed to bring about as a statesman in 1848. Having upset the government of his canton, as the leader of the democratic revolution of 1846, he became its first magistrate in the following year. As such, he drafted the instructions of the Geneva delegation to the Diet. These expressly called for not only the summoning of a constituent assembly and the opposition to an unitary constitution, but also, alone of all cantonal instruction, the promotion of "a happy combination of the federal democratic element to be represented in a Chamber elected on the basis of the population and of the constitutional element represented in a second Chamber where the states should all enjoy equal representation."[114]

Between 1831, when the American precedent first came to be proposed by individual orators and writers, and 1848, when the federal Diet finally decided that Switzerland should follow it by incorporating provisions to that effect in the new constitution, it was ever in the public eye. But it was never truly popular. Those who had the courage to advocate its imitation, once its imitation had ceased to be a mere day dream, as it had been before 1830, were looked upon as academic Utopians. Even among the radical extremists, for many of whom a unitary state with a single popular chamber was the aim, bicameral federalism was not in favor.

Thus we read in an account of a meeting of the Swiss Security Society held in Zofingen on February 26, 1834, that a speech by Kasthofer, in which he advocated the establishment

[112] *Europe centrale,* January 3, 1835.

[113] *Ibid.,* January 10, 29, 31 and February 5, 14 and 19.

[114] *Mémorial des séances du Grand Conseil du 24 septembre 1847 au 1er novembre 1848* (Geneva, 1848), vol. 1, p. 55.

of two chambers, "one of representatives of the people and the other of the government" was "not appreciated."[115]

The popular agitation in favor of the American system continued unabated, however. It was carried on by the publication of pamphlets and newspaper articles and also by the organization of public meetings. One of the most important of these was a gathering of the liberal "Nationalverein" held at Langenthal in the canton of Berne on September 23, 1838. Theodor Mundt, a German traveller who witnessed it, tells us how, under the chairmanship of Kasthofer, over 8,000 Swiss citizens met in the open air on that occasion and in spite of a violent rainstorm listened, in religious silence, to a series of speeches in favor of constitutional reform, of which the most impressive was one by Dr. Troxler. In his interesting account, we read:

As I gathered from personal conversations with several members of the "Nationalverein," they had taken as a model North American constitutional institutions and had especially before their eyes the bicameral system of Congress.[116]

The campaign in favor of the American system, of which we have mentioned some striking early instances and which continued until 1848, had obviously not succeeded in overcoming the deep-rooted popular prejudice against it. Yet the efforts of its friends had not been vain, as the events of 1848 were shortly to show.

Let us now once more revert to the constitutional debates as they were conducted on the official plane before the Diet by the plenipotentiaries of the twenty-two cantons.

Although the Rossi Pact of 1832 and the revised draft of 1833 had both been discarded, the resolution of July 17, 1832, still stood. A majority of cantons had then decided on the revision of the Pact of 1815. As long as that decision was not formally reversed, the question of constitutional reform remained on the agenda of the Diet. So it was that year after year, in each successive ordinary session of the Diet from 1834 until 1847, the cantonal delegates, meeting in July or August in Lucerne, Zurich or Berne were called upon to consider the matter.

In fact the undertaking appeared almost hopeless. According to the most approved legal opinion, the Pact of 1815

[115] *Journal de Genève*, March 1, 1834, p. 3.
[116] Mundt, *op. cit.*, p. 146.

could be revised only by the concordant will of all the members of the Diet or at least, on the proposal of a majority of its members, by the concordant will of all the cantons represented. But not only was such a unanimity always out of the question, but no constructive proposal ever even met with the approval of a clear majority of delegates at the Diet.

Very soon the most conservative cantons,—Uri, Schwyz, Unterwalden, Neuchâtel and Basle-City, and from time to time one or another of the others—proposed that the matter should be dropped entirely.[117] They, however, never polled more than 6 or 7 votes in favor of their proposal.

At the other extreme, the larger cantons—Berne, Zurich, Saint-Gall, Aargau, Thurgau, and from year to year one or another of the others—proposed to refer the problem to a popularly elected constituent assembly. But although that also would have entailed the relief of the Diet, this radical proposal, when it came to a vote before that body, was even less successful than that of the extreme conservatives.

The remaining cantons were equally opposed to the indefinite postponement of the revision of the federal constitution and to its consideration by a popularly elected constituent assembly. They realized that to consent to such a postponement was to maintain the state of affairs which was fast becoming impossible. It was threatening the unity and even the integrity of the country. And it was intolerable for all law-abiding citizens, as the Pact of 1815 was being respected neither by those who would not nor by those who would but could not amend it. But these cantons realized also that to consent to the summoning of a constituent assembly was to sacrifice their local sovereignty and to jeopardize the federal structure of the country. This also was a very real peril. Certain of the spokesmen of the larger Protestant cantons, and especially of Berne, the largest of them all, did not always disguise their intention of using the constituent assembly as a means of setting up a unitary state.[118]

Although there was disagreement enough in the Diet on points of secondary importance, it was on the fundamental issue of the structure of the state and consequently on the mode of federal representation that the deadlock was the most

[117] Cf. for instance *Abschied*, 1835, p. 160; 1836, p. 93.
[118] Cf. for instance *Abschied*, 1834, p. 68.

ominous and the most continuous. The smaller cantons which, of course, constituted a majority, as they included both those of the first and of the third group, would not hear of any form of representation in the national legislature which would subject them to a will not their own. And the governments of the larger cantons, representing a majority of the Swiss population, more and more resolutely opposed any reform which would result in the possible subjection of that popular majority to the will of a popular minority, represented by a majority of cantonal governments.

What is surprising under these circumstances is not that the American precedent should from time to time have been invoked, but rather that, being familiar to all, it should not have been more frequently and more fully discussed. What is less surprising, given the inevitable conservatism of a body such as the Diet, is that it should have been followed only after fifteen years of sterile debate and then only as the result of a revolution!

A careful perusal of the *Abschiede* or *Recès* of the Diet, as its official records are called in German and in French, reveals but very few references to the American example. These records, it is true, are often so summary that it does not follow that no more such references actually occurred in the debates. In fact, the first very vague mention of America I discovered therein after 1833 tends to prove the contrary.

On July 28, 1835, in the course of the annual exchange of views on constitutional reform, we read in the official proceedings of the Diet:

Illustrations of the various proposals outlined were on this occasion quoted from the history of federations in the old and in the new world.[119]

It so happened that in 1835, Lucerne was represented at the Diet by Casimir Pfyffer, the same politician who had published the famous *Appeal to the Vorort* at the beginning of 1831 which we mentioned above. As I discovered in a bibliography that the speech Pfyffer delivered that day at the Diet had been published *in extenso* as a pamphlet, I thought it worth while to seek to consult the latter document. I was rewarded by finding therein the following statements:

[119] *Abschied*, 1835, p. 158.

Even if we discard, as we must, the idea of a unitary constitution, there is no reason not to seek otherwise to promote the general interests of Switzerland by tightening the bonds of our federation and by strengthening the central authority. This can be achieved by substituting for the present loose association a federal state about on the North American model. . . . As the state constitutions of North America, so our cantonal constitutions rest almost without exception on the basis of popular sovereignty. Therefore no interest of any privileged class can any longer oppose the strengthening of the federal bond. A federal state, on the model of the American, would offer the essential advantage of permitting the peoples of the various cantons to enjoy their local legislative and administrative autonomy while entrusting the defense of the general interests of Switzerland to federal organs, as to the truly supreme authorities of the country.[120]

In 1840, the Diet sought to break the persisting deadlock by setting up among its members a conference to consider the possibility of amending at least those provisions of the Pact of 1815 which dealt with the organization of the Vorort and the Diet as central authorities. In this less formal gathering, in which the delegates could more freely voice their own personal opinions than in the full Diet, Landammann Baumgartner of Saint-Gall declared in his own name that, if called upon to choose between "unitarism" and "federalism," he would prefer the latter. But he added that he would favor a new form of federalism. As a national legislature, he would set up a "Swiss Great Council," of about 100 members, elected in the cantons proportionally to their population. The decisions of this body, however, in so far as they affected the individual cantons, would be valid only if and when the latter had expressly ratified them. Such a ratification could be secured by correspondence, unless, he added, "One preferred to set up a special legislature corresponding to the Senate of the United States of North America in which the twenty-two cantons would be represented."[121]

Druey, who attended the conference as representative of the canton of Vaud, when discussing this suggestion observed

[120] *Reden über die schweizerische Bundesreform* von Appellations-Gerichts-Präsident Doctor Casimir Pfyffer, Gesandter des Standes Luzern (Bern, 1835), pp. 12-13.

[121] *Abschied*, 1840, Beilage Litt. Q, p. 4.

that it would be difficult to introduce the bicameral system in Switzerland without also setting up a very strong executive.[122]

The result of the conference of 1840 was a report submitted to the Diet of 1841. Expressing a minority opinion, Druey and Casimir Pfyffer of Lucerne observed in this report:

As for the organization of the federal authorities, the most adequate solution considered in itself might well be a combination of representation according to population with an equal represen- tation of all the cantons. But such a scheme, which would resem- ble the bicameral system as practiced in the United States of North America, would hardly prove acceptable in Switzerland, were it only on account of the number of representatives and of the correspondingly high cost involved. Therefore, it might be wise to apply the same principle in a simplified form.[123]

Druey and Pfyffer therefore recommended the establishment of a single chamber with unequal representation of the unequal cantons. As this solution was no more acceptable to the small cantons than the maintenance of the existing system to the larger ones, the Diet, once again, adjourned without breaking the deadlock.

THE DRAFTING OF THE CONSTITUTION OF 1848, 1847-1848

The discussions dragged on until the summer of 1847 when a civil war broke out in Switzerland. The opposing parties were no longer the "unitarians" and the "federalists" but, as was observed in the Diet "the friends and the foes of the con- vents and of the Jesuits."[124] However, as in the American Civil War, where the real issue was likewise elsewhere, the Swiss conflict also presented a constitutional aspect.

In the Diet of 1847, the Protestant majority was alone repre- sented to the exclusion of the members of the clerical "Sonder- bund" or secessionists.[125] Realizing that this circumstance would facilitate the solution of a problem which the latters' secession had rendered more urgent than ever, it was decided by a ma- jority of 13 votes to make the most of the opportunity. Ac-

[122] Ibid., p. 5.
[123] Abschied, 1841, Beilage Litt. S, p. 2.
[124] Abschied, 1847, p. 82.
[125] For a full history of Swiss constitutional evolution during this period, cf. my L'individu et l'Etat, pp. 270-301.

cordingly a committe of the Diet, in which all the participating cantons were to have one representative, was set up and instructed to submit to the Diet itself the draft of a revised federal constitution.[126] In the discussion preceding this decision the records of the Diet contain only a fleeting reference to the American precedent.[127]

When the committee met for its first session on February 17, 1848, the *Sonderbund* had been beaten in the field after a brief and very unequal military struggle. Consequently all the defeated and more or less sincerely penitent cantons except two came to be represented on the committee. Its task was not, however, rendered much more difficult by that circumstance. All wished to endow the country with a new constitution. Everyone realized that it was now or never. And no one relished the thought of pursuing indefinitely the debates which had begun in 1831 and had never been truly interrupted since. In consequence, the members of the committee, although of course informed of the mind of their respective governments, were not bound by any hard and fast instructions, as had always been the case in the Diet. Moreover, as all were eager to reach agreement and almost all were anxious to strengthen the federal bond, they were less reluctant than they had ever been in the past to make some sacrifice of local interests and prejudices.

It is not easy exactly to follow the course of the debates in the constituent committee. It met in private and at its first sitting adopted a resolution to the effect that no minutes should be kept in which the names of the speakers would appear.[128]

This self-denying decision, which undoubtedly made for shorter speeches and for readier conciliation, is as embarrassing for the historian as it was wise. To guide one through the anonymous and very summary records, such as they are, and through the report of the committee, which was drafted by Druey, of Vaud and Kern, of Thurgau,[129] one has but the rather scanty memoirs and correspondence of some of the individual members. The manuscript notes of Frey-Herosé, the delegate

[126] *Abschied*, 1847, p. 82.

[127] *Ibid.*, p. 79.

[128] *Protocole des Délibérations de la Commission chargée, le 16 août 1847, par la Haute Diète fédérale, de la revision du Pacte fédéral du 7 août 1815*, p. 2.

[129] *Rapport de la Commission qui a élaboré le projet de la Constitution fédérale du 8 avril 1848* (Lausanne, 1848).

for Aargau, and of Jonas Furrer, of Zurich, which have been carefully analyzed by recent writers[130] and which I have consulted myself in the federal record office,[131] are particularly valuable in this respect.

What we learn from these sources, however inadequate for other purposes, is quite sufficient to allow us to realize one central fact; namely that the structure of the new federal state and particularly of its legislature constituted the cardinal problem and the one which it took the committee most time, effort and sacrifice to solve.

After some discussion on the source of sovereignty, which the representatives of the larger cantons tended to locate in the Swiss people and most of their colleagues in the constituent cantons, the committee tackled what was in fact but another aspect of the same fundamental question: How and by whom was Switzerland to be governed?

In a preliminary encounter, the friends and the foes of the existing Diet once again confronted the arguments they had been exchanging ever since 1831. Geneva and Lucerne alone seem to have favored the bicameral system.[132] Jonas Furrer, the very influential representative of Zurich on the commission was biased against that system because, as he wrote in his own notes:

I confess to some difficulty in repressing the *Timeo Danaos et dona ferentes* in considering the bicameral proposals, when I see that these proposals were first put forward by the ultra-radicals and by the extreme conservatives.[133]

A first vote was taken at the beginning of the session. As neither side had a clear majority, 9 members being in favor of the maintainance of the Diet and 11 proposing some form of national legislature, the prospects of agreement seemed decidedly dark. Thereupon by a majority of 14 votes, the matter was referred to a sub-committee of 7.[134]

In this preliminary discussion, the only mention of the American precedent in the official records is the following:

[130] Cf. particularly Hans Schmid, *Bundesrat Frey-Herosé*, Aarau, 1917 and René van Berchem, *De la Chambre unique au système bicaméral* (Genève, 1924), both of which contain ample bibliographies.

[131] Cf. *Archives fédérales* 17 a (Furrer) and 17 b (Frey-Herosé).

[132] *Archives fédérales*, 17 a, pp. 5, 110.

[133] *Ibid.*, p. 107.

[134] *Protocole, op. cit.*, pp. 9 et seq., 74 et seq.

One member . . . states that the bicameral system that has been suggested, is borrowed from North America where it had been established on the basis of the English constitution; that this system is in no way adapted to the entirely different circumstances of the Swiss cantons. In order to reëstablish the national unity, broken up by the existence of two Chambers, there had been created in the United States an administrative power endowed with so wide an executive authority that it could never become popular in Switzerland.[135]

On March 19, 1848, the sub-committee of 7, of whose discussion there is no detailed record, presented its report. It would be more accurate to speak of its findings, inasmuch as its members were far from unanimous, a majority opinion being opposed by two distinct minorities. However, on one essential point, all of its members agreed: "the supreme authority of the Confederation" was to be "exercised by a federal assembly" composed of "two sections, namely: a. of the Council of Representatives; b. of the Diet."[136]

Thus the bicameral system, which no one seemed to have championed with any ardor before the full committee, was, less than a fortnight later, unanimously recommended by a subcommittee composed of 7 of the former's most influential members!

Nothing more clearly reveals the true origin of what in Switzerland had now long been called "the American system." That origin is to be found, not indeed in its natural popularity, but on the contrary, in spite of its real lack of popularity, in its inherent merits as a compromise between two radically opposed and otherwise mutually exclusive forms of organization. In the report of the subcommittee, no express mention is made of the American precedent. The bicameral proposal is explained as being, not indeed welcome, but at least acceptable to both friends and foes of the existing system.[137]

When the sub-committee's proposal came to a vote before the full committee, the results were as follows:

a) for a single chamber: 10 votes

[135] *Ibid.*, p. 83.
[136] *Ibid.*, p. 103.
[137] *Ibid.*, p. 107. *Cf. Archives fédérales,* 17 a, pp. 167 *et seq.;* 17 b, pp. 82 *et seq.*

b) for a representation of the national and of the cantonal principles: 11 votes.

c) for two separate chambers: 6 votes

d) for the sub-committee's proposal: 17 votes[138]

On the second reading of its draft on April 5, 1848, the committee ratified its previous decision. It decided by 13 votes to call the Council of Representatives the National Council, and by 20 to call the Diet the Council of States.

Commenting on its proposals in its report, the committee stated:

The example of the United States and of the other countries which have two legislative chambers allays the fears expressed that such a scheme might lead to continuous conflicts and to systematic antagonism between them . . .

Admittedly Switzerland is in many respects very different from the United States of America; but as the task of governing that vast federation is much more complicated and difficult than that of governing the Swiss Confederation, the success made of the experiment of two chambers in that part of the world for more than sixty years past allows us *a fortiori* to hope that it will also prove suitable to our country.[139]

The report goes on to admit that the running of the bicameral system will undoubtedly prove expensive. But it pleads that there should be "ample compensation for the enhanced costs," if the Confederation be thereby well governed.

As for the other American idea, that of a popularly elected president, it is in the report dismissed in the following terms:

Without ignoring the advantages which such a presidential office would present for the unity, continuity and responsibility of administration and also as an expression of national solidarity, the committee could not consider proposing an institution so contrary to the ideas and habits of Switzerland. It might have appeared to be a step on the road to monarchy or to dictatorship.[140]

Instead of being first submitted to the full Diet, the draft of the committee was communicated directly to the cantonal governments. This somewhat irregular procedure was followed in order to allow them to instruct their delegates as to the at-

---

[138] *Ibid.*, p. 117.
[139] *Rapport, op. cit.*, p. 60.
[140] *Ibid.*, p. 65.

titude they should adopt with respect to it and thus to gain time. Fortunately for the survival of the draft, these instructions were generally formulated without any of that aggressive obstinacy which had formerly characterized them. All cantonal governments realized that if, on the morrow of a bloody civil war, the Diet was to reject, or even seriously to amend, the project which had been most carefully drafted and thus to tamper with agreements that had been most precariously reached by their delegates, all hope of constitutional reform would have to be abandoned or at least indefinitely postponed.

As the modifications undergone by the draft of the committee, as a result of the debates of the final Diet of 1848, were very slight, the instructions of the delegates to that body present only an historical interest for our purpose. They do, however, very helpfully enlighten us on the official state of mind which they reflect.

In his above-quoted book, M. René van Berchem notes the results of his careful investigations into cantonal archives and parliamentary records on this point. These results are such as to authorize us to divide the cantons into three groups according to their views on the bicameral, that is on the American, solution of the Swiss federal problem.[141]

The first of these groups, composed of the four French-speaking cantons of Geneva, Vaud, Neuchâtel and Fribourg as well as of Lucerne and Solothurn, welcomed that solution as the best conceivable under the circumstances. For Geneva alone, it is true, the triumph of the American system was also a cantonal victory, no other cantonal delegation besides that instructed by the government of James Fazy having been pledged to it since 1847. M. van Berchem tentatively attributes the attitude of the French-speaking cantons to a less general reluctance to follow foreign constitutional examples. Was it not due also to the greater desire of a linguistic minority to be spared the enhanced centralization which would have been implied by the most probable alternative, namely that of a unicameral legislature, elected on a democratic basis? Our explanation does certainly not apply to Fribourg. The government of that profoundly Catholic canton far more faithfully represented its victorious radical minority than its defeated

[141] van Berchem, op. cit., pp. 197 et seq.

and artificially dethroned conservative majority. But it would seem to account for the position of the other three.

The political situation in Lucerne was similar to that in Fribourg on the morrow of the downfall of the *Sonderbund*. As for Solothurn, her instructions were undoubtedly influenced, if not dictated, by her chief delegate, Landammann Munzinger. As an old personal disciple of Dr. Troxler, this popular magistrate had struggled valiantly in favor of the American system in the committee as well as in his own canton after he had been converted to it in the sub-committee.[142]

The majority of the liberal German-Swiss delegates, including those of Berne and Zurich, were instructed to vote in the first instance for a unicameral federal legislature in which representation would be more or less proportional to population. They were authorized, as a second choice, to accept the bicameral solution, but only as a makeshift and in order to avoid a renewed deadlock.

As for the three primitive cantons of Uri, Schwyz and Unterwalden, which had constituted the backbone of the opposition to all reform ever since 1831, their position—as also that of Schaffhausen, Appenzell and Basle-City—was the exact reverse. The larger liberal cantons purchased the National Council, in which their superior population assured them of leadership, and even of predominance, at the price of a Council of States, in which they were outnumbered by their smaller rivals. The latter on the other hand reluctantly resigned themselves to the establishment of the National Council, in the hope that their dearly cherished Diet might be perpetuated in the Council of States and that they might there hold in check the dangerous ambitions of the former.

The last debate on the bicameral system, which took place at the Diet on May 16, 1848, need not detain us long. Although the acceptance of the system was a foregone conclusion, the opposition to it was all the more remarkable. The official record refers to this opposition in the following terms:

It is true that in favor of the bicameral system, one could point to the example of other nations and especially of republican North America, which under this system felt perfectly free and

<hr/>

142 J. J. Blumer, *Handbuch des Schweizerischen Bundesstaatsrechtes*, vol. I 3rd ed. (Basle 1891), p. 151; Cf. *Archives fédérales*, 17 a, pp. 100, 171, 176; Secretan, *Troxler, loc. cit.*, p. 124.

happy and where the legislative power was exercised by two houses in almost all the states. However, even leaving aside the fact that the North American states have inherited the bicameral system as a tradition from their mother country, one should take into account the peculiarity of each state and of each nation. Now in Switzerland that system enjoyed no popularity whatever, because the people were accustomed to associate the idea of legislation with one authority only, be it the Landsgemeinde or the Great Council.[143]

The only mention of the United States, made in the course of the arguments presented in favor of the American system, occurs in the following passage of the official record:

The example of other states, especially of North America, proves that it was possible to maintain a good and strong government under the bicameral system. In the North American Union, it has imposed itself by reason of internal necessities and it had not at all prevailed as a mere copy of the institutions of old England. The historical evolution of the genesis of the United States constitution showed this very clearly.[144]

When it came to a vote on the same day, the bicameral system was accepted by a majority of 13 cantons and then, after none of the other proposals had secured more than 5 votes, it was finally adopted by 16 cantons, including Berne and Zurich which, with the impenitent primitive cantons, had led the struggle against it heretofore.

After 26 sittings, the draft constitution was adopted by the Diet, on June 27, 1848. Again 13½ cantons voted in its favor; 7½ abstained, Schwyz alone cast a negative vote.

The draft was then submitted to the cantons for ratification. According to their various constitutions, it was considered by their legislatures, by their popular electorates, or by both. The results were communicated to the Diet which, on September 4, 1848, set up a special committee to report on them. According to the report of this committee, the draft had been adopted by 15½ cantons and rejected by 6½, the former representing a population of 1,898,887 inhabitants and the latter one of 292,371.[145]

These results were held to be unexpectedly favorable by the friends of the new constitution. Accordingly, the Diet de-

[143] *Abschied*, 1848, p. 43.
[144] *Ibid.*, p. 49.
[145] Rappard, *op. cit.*, p. 272.

cided to put it into force as of September 12, 1848. The three original cantons of Uri, Schwyz und Unterwalden alone protested that such action was unconstitutional as, they declared: ". . . The former federal organization rested on a contractual basis and consequently could not be legally revised except by the concurrent will of all the cantons."[146]

Thus, less patient and less fortunate than their American predecessors, the fathers of the present Swiss constitution did not succeed in securing a unanimous decision in favor of their proposal. That it was imposed on an unwilling minority on the morrow of a military defeat, is a fact not without historical significance. In most federal referendum votes, ever since, the cantons which rejected the constitution of 1848 have polled negative popular majorities.

Nevertheless, no responsible Swiss statesman today, even in those cantons, really regrets the conditions prevailing before its adoption. The situation may be compared with that in the United States where, I am assured, no responsible statesman, even in the South, today, deplores the abolition of slavery. In both countries, there is perhaps still some sorrowful sentimental longing for what has "gone with the wind." But no one would seriously welcome the return of the former constitutional conditions, which were obviously incompatible with the national interest.

One must note on the contrary how quickly and deeply the "American system" took root in Swiss soil. Neither in its federalism nor in its bicameral institutions had that system any precedent in the previous history of the country. Still, even today, when under the pressure of foreign events an upheaval has taken place and a state of intellectual turmoil been created in which such fundamental values as political liberty and democracy themselves are challenged, no one has ventured to question the soundness of the federal structure set up in 1848.

This striking fact establishes Switzerland's constitutional debt to the United States for the present of bicameral federalism. That the Swiss people did not welcome the American gift with that enthusiastic alacrity with which a child snatches an attractive toy from the hands of its parents on its birthday, these pages have made abundantly clear. As we have seen, their attitude was rather that of an infant most reluctantly swallow-

[146] *Abschied*, 1848, II, p. 68.

ing a strange and unsavory medicine, after he had long sought, but entirely failed, to find relief from his troubles in more familiar household remedies. But, although the Swiss people thus took the drug in spite, rather than on account, of its foreign origin, they were undoubtedly encouraged thereto by the example of the Americans whom it had permanently cured of an ailment similar to their own sixty years before. This circumstance and especially the fact that it has proved decisively and lastingly salutary at home, fully suffices to explain and to justify the debt of gratitude the Swiss people owe their American friends for its discovery.

CONCLUSION

The story of how the United States, by the force of her example, contributed to the conversion of Switzerland to the principles of bicameral federalism, devised in Philadelphia in 1787, thus reaches its normal conclusion. It has been told with sufficient detail to be fastidious, I fear, but also, I venture to hope, with sufficient clarity to be enlightening. Its special historical interest is limited to the two democracies concerned and, even within their boundaries, is hardly such as to suggest any headlines that might startle the general public.

What is of universal interest, however, is the lesson it teaches, the political lesson of how general union can be combined with local freedom. That lesson, which the disunited nations of the world have still to learn from the United States of America, as the since united cantons of Switzerland learned it from them nearly a century ago, is one of peculiarly tragic timeliness today. That it has long been understood to be one of world importance, is shown by a statement made more than seventy years ago by my fellow-countryman Professor Rüttimann. In the preface of his monumental comparative study of American and Swiss constitutional practice, he wrote:

The North American Union at present unites about forty states of quite unequal size and power in a community of law from which not only war, but also every other form of self-help, has been excluded as entirely dispensable. Likewise in small Switzerland, which was formerly decried as the seat of constant anarchy and wild discord, the federal state has since 1848 justified itself as a foundation on which the citizens of twenty-five cantons, in spite of their diversity of speech, of faith, of political views and of material interests, have been able to live together in happy and ordered circumstances and to develop in common a gratifying prosperity.

If mankind is perfectible and capable of constant progress, Europe will also sooner or later come to see that its peoples are one to another as members of one body; that the solidarity between them is real; that every wound inflicted upon one of them spares none of the others; that any conflict between them is susceptible of a peaceful settlement. Then they also will unite into one federal state and come to look upon our present international law in much the same light as that in which we today look upon the mediaeval law of reprisals.[147]

These words, written on the morrow of the American Civil War may well serve as a conclusion to this monograph, prepared during the present world civil war. What was true two generations ago is assuredly no less true today. Why should the hopes which a study of Swiss-American institutions suggested to a Swiss scholar in 1867 be forbidden to his successor in 1940? And why should they not be shared by friends of peace and liberty everywhere, whatever their national allegiance?

I had just put the final touch to these pages when my eye chanced upon a remarkable article in the July number of the *Annals of the American Academy of Political and Social Science*. The author, Mr. Ralph W. Page of Philadelphia, concludes as follows his study on *Designs for a World Order*:

It is to be hoped and expected that universal exposition and discussion will prepare the people of the world for some such miracle as happened in Philadelphia in 1787.

May this message from the Geneva home of Albert Gallatin, to the state of Pennsylvania in which that "minister of peace," as he called himself at the end of his long career, first found a welcome in America, be accepted as a modest contribution to that necessary "universal exposition and discussion"!

[147] Rüttimann, *op. cit.*, vol. I, p. VI.

Minorities in American History

By

ARTHUR C. COLE, Ph.D.*

THE topic, "Minorities in American History," sounds a modern
note which, projected back over the three hundred years of
the nation's past, summons an array of familiar facts for review
in terms of present-day interest. For one thing, there is the
obvious factor of nationality groups and their rôles.[1] A country
whose peopling has drawn upon the offerings of almost every
corner of Europe may well hesitate to label as a minority any
group which has contributed to the human resources of the
nation. Yet, any problem in this field that may exist today
had its counterpart in the past in circumstances where well-
defined groups revealed an element of cultural, if not political,
isolation which challenged the attention of more dominant
forces, an attention the implications of which its objects were
in turn forced to recognize.

During the period of over three centuries that the stream of
population has flowed to these shores, three main elements have
been defined: (1) the Anglo-Saxon contribution from Britain,
earmarked by the traditions of empire as the dominant group,
(2) a conglomerate mass of peasants, burghers, and even revolutionary dreamers and intellectuals who for divers reasons left
their various native lands to find homes in the New World,
knowing that the culture of those parts was sufficiently established in the Anglo-Saxon pattern to make them feel a
sense of their own alien status, and (3) accretions to the British
Empire—and to the republic later carved out of it—of alien
peoples as parts of the fruits of territorial conquest or of the
transfer of territory by purchase treaty. Out of these elements

* Professor and chairman of the Division of History, Western Reserve University.

[1] The term "minorities" has no definite status in American history. Witness
its absence from the recent *Dictionary of American History* (New York, 1940).
Sectional groups made conscious of their minority status are as properly covered by the term. See Jesse T. Carpenter, *The South as a Conscious Minority,
1789-1861* (New York, 1930). Political groups experiencing more than a temporary relegation to opposition status are also covered by such a label.

a republic famed as a land of opportunity has sought to forge
a united nation. That this process has involved less of the melting pot and more of the mixing bowl is a commonplace among
historians. Withal, however, the course of American history as
well as recent trends properly raises the question how far the
various "alien" elements have sought the preservation and
orderly array of their respective "rights" and cultures in separate compartments, and to what extent these forces have been
allowed the status of self-conscious minorities entitled to
such rights.

To the degree that minority population elements came into
the American picture by the normal course of immigration
to a new land of opportunity which welcomed new arrivals with
open arms, there would seem to be little element of a problem
of national minorities. From almost the beginning, indeed,
colonial proprietors—both regal and vice-regal—found that
their welcome to all comers varied largely in direct ratio to
their ability to reap a harvest from the land sales that would
ensue. The story of American settlement by non-English stocks
is largely the story of the exploitation of such opportunities by
proprietors and of the resulting assimilation—however gradual
—of these elements into the American scheme of things. Distinctive local color and distinctive contributions to the American way of life did not of necessity mean a minorities problem.
French Huguenots, Irish, Scotch-Irish, Germans, Swiss, Swedes,
Finns, and others entered the American mixing bowl, only to
find that it later became an inevitable melting pot.

Group interest and independence were almost inevitably
reenforced by superficial distinctions in language and culture.
Temporarily at least these interests were likely to connote a
common political motivation and to induce common political
action. Dreams of a consolidated German state in the New
World were almost a perennial concomitant of emigration from
the fatherland. The realities of immigrant life, however, forced
associations with other groups including the older stocks, with
the result that separatism yielded to broader and more powerful
forces. A new and distinctive conception of citizenship, which
assumed that allegiance that was the accidental circumstance
of birth would readily yield to one based upon personal choice,
served as a powerful agency making for integration. Only
when the "foreign group," individually or collectively. grew

to numbers that were deemed menacing to the majority, or when group interest and independence were preserved in a spirit of clannish ultra-self-sufficiency, did the normal course of assimilation in the new world culture seem to be defied, in which case a natural inspiration of defensive nativism arose among the more established elements.

Whatever problems these nationality groups raised date back to colonial days and from the viewpoint of voluntary immigration seem to have found a focus in Pennsylvania. While several other colonies had, qualitatively, as heterogeneous a population, few of them felt any real challenge in the presence of these outlanders. When Penn and his agents opened their doors with every element of enthusiasm that it was possible for shrewd realists to display, there rushed to a province already populated by blocks of non-English stocks a mass of thrifty German peasants seeking refuge from the poverty, tyranny, and religious intolerance of a fatherland that had been blighted and demoralized, first by a succession of religious and civil wars that had swept over Central Europe, and later by the operations of Louis XIV in the Rhineland.[2]

With motives that varied from bread-and-butter necessity to utopian idealism, a great stream of population poured into the counties west of Philadelphia, with an overflow that in time trickled far down the Cumberland and Shenandoah Valleys. Subsidiary currents flowed to other ports of entry and thence in turn into the great American back-country. Essentially represented by the group known in popular parlance as the "Pennsylvania Dutch," this German stock soon won respect and admiration for a thrifty and highly efficient, diversified farming that made its settlements veritable garden-spots in the wilderness.[3]

Trading oppression in its many forms for such fruits of labor, these colonists willingly became the subjects of a foreign power. At first, however, political allegiance was really a matter of little importance to them. Having lost a paradise in the Old World, many had been aroused by glowing accounts of utopian opportunity in the New World to seek to achieve

[2] Oscar Kuhns, *The German and Swiss Settlements of Colonial Pennsylvania: A Study of the So-Called Pennsylvania Dutch* (New York, 1901), 24-27.

[3] Richard H. Shryock, "British versus German Traditions in Colonial Agriculture," *Mississippi Valley Historical Review*, XXVI (1939), 47-48; Carl Wittke, *We Who Built America* (New York, 1940), 80-82.

personal "Kingdoms of Paradise"—as Christian Priber called his communistic venture with Cherokee Indians—on American soil. "Every man a king" was an established slogan for an American utopia over two hundred years before it was popularized by a twentieth-century demagogue. In due time these would-be monarchs were content to have a hand in the founding of a new nation wherein advocates of further German immigration could depict "13 golden gates . . . open to the victims of intolerance and despotism."[4]

This Pennsylvania Dutch contribution to American life was only challenged by a fear, expressed by Governor George Keith as early as 1717, that the German element—which soon came to number one-third of the population—would inundate the colony of Pennsylvania.[5] Revived by large arrivals a decade later, this alarm led to an official policy of requiring the newcomers to be registered and to sign a declaration of allegiance and subjection to the King of England and of fidelity to the proprietary of Pennsylvania. Even this did not allay the concern of Benjamin Franklin. "Why should *Pennsylvania*, founded by the *English*, become a Colony of *Aliens*, who will shortly be so numerous as to Germanize us, instead of our Anglifying them, and will never adopt our Language or Customs any more than they can acquire our Complexion?" he rather peevishly asked in 1751.[6]

Two years later Franklin repeated his fears of the Germans outnumbering the English element. Not questioning their exemplary industry and frugality and their excellence as "Husbandmen" who contributed "greatly to the Improvement of a Country," he proposed as the solution of the problem, "to distribute them more equally, mix them with the English, establish English Schools, where they are now too thick settled."[7] The practical operation of this plan was precluded by circumstances, and the history of the Pennsylvania Dutch, per-

[4] Verner W. Crane, "A Lost Utopia on the American Frontier," *Sewanee Review*, XXVII (1919), 50-58; Michael Kraus, "America and the Utopian Ideal in the Eighteenth Century," *Mississippi Valley Historical Review*, XXII (1936), 492, 496, 499.

[5] Kuhns, *op. cit.*, 54, 55, 58. Kuhns's estimate agrees with that of Benjamin Franklin to a committee of the House of Commons in 1776. See Wittke, *op. cit.*, 71, quoting *German-American Annals*, VI (1903), 256.

[6] Albert H. Smyth, ed., *The Writings of Benjamin Franklin* (New York, 1905-1907), III, 72.

[7] *Ibid.*, III, 141.

sistently clinging to their own manners and customs, shows their assimilation, at least culturally, working out only after a long period of time.

On the political side Franklin stated his opinion that "Measures of great Temper" were necessary in dealing with the Germans lest, he said, "through their Indiscretion, or ours, or both, great Disorders may one day arise among us." "They behave, however," he went on, "submissively enough at present to the civil Government, which I wish they may continue to do, for I remember when they modestly declined intermeddling in our Elections, but now they come in Droves and carry all before them, except in one or two counties."[8] Since he was here, in part, referring to the conscientious scruples of the German sectarians against politics as well as against military matters, it may be questioned whether much self-conscious political activity was actually in the picture.

It was true, as Franklin pointed out, that the German colonists used their own language not only in every-day life, but in legal and judicial transactions. He even ventured the opinion that interpreters might soon "be necessary in the Assembly, to tell one half of our Legislators what the other half say." The danger of inadequate political control seemed the greater because, he said, "few of the English understand the German language, and so cannot address them either from the Press or Pulpit."[9] Wherefore, to direct their thinking on political issues, he set up a German newspaper of his own, the *Philadelphische Zeitung*.

There seems to have been little evidence to warrant Franklin's fear of the Germans coming to an understanding with the French enemy on the frontier, or of any other large-scale intrigues or influences. In general, their early activities were limited to local and county politics. Later, when their leaders came more prominently into the political life of the state, their interests were seldom confined to those of their own group. They became increasingly active in frontier defense, in the support of the American revolutionary cause, and in the movement for the adoption of the Constitution in 1787.[10] One index

[8] *Ibid.*, III, 139-140.
[9] *Ibid.*, 139, 140.
[10] Kuhns, *op. cit.*, 195-215. In the convention of 1776, of which Franklin was president, 22 of the 96 delegates were Germans. *Ibid.*, 208.

of these interests, perhaps, may have been the vote in 1786 of the Pennsylvania legislature to have its *Journal* and other official documents printed in German translation.[11] Later, despite the devotion of the Pennsylvania Dutch to their own parochial schools, it was under a governor of their own stock, George Wolf, that the free public school law was duly enacted in 1834.

The early Pennsylvania Dutch problem might well have been prophetic of the situation that was to arise when the nation a century later witnessed a great tide of immigration flowing to nearly all its shores. In time the processes that made for assimilation, usually well advanced in the second generation, achieved the acculturation and political absorption of these foreign immigrants, overwhelming though the stream seemed at many stages.

The immigrants, to be sure, brought with them their own cultural interests, such as the *Biergarten*, the *Turnverein*, the choral societies and rifle clubs of the Germans; but they also quickly took up American ways and formed their own Odd Fellow lodges, and even tribes of German Red Men. Still more important, they did much to mellow the sterner Puritanical influences that surrounded them and convinced many that German *Gemütlichkeit* might well temper Yankee stiffness and repression. The political objectives that they brought from Europe were usually revolutionary plans to redeem the homeland from autocratic rule, plans that were shortly dropped for more active identification with the prevailing currents of American politics.[12] Indeed, even the interventionism that was so actively stimulated by the visit of Louis Kossuth in 1851 was a political objective normally voiced through the orthodox channel of Democratic party politics.

The mid-nineteenth century stream of Irish immigrants did not fail to produce its problems. These sons of Erin invaded a New England which had long boasted of its homogeneous population, and began the penetration of that section by alien groups which have, politically as well as socially, forced a defensive attitude upon the scions of the original Anglo-American stock. They added strength everywhere to a church the growth

[11] Wittke, *op. cit.*, 88.
[12] Arthur C. Cole, *The Irrepressible Conflict*, Arthur M. Schlesinger and Dixon R. Fox, eds., *A History of American Life*, VII (New York, 1934), 135-139.

of which was under violent attack from forces centering in New England Puritanism. Their dreams of freedom for Ireland achieved with their aid, led to their continued organization on nationalist lines—moderately, at first, in the Hibernian societies, and militantly, later, in the Fenian brotherhood. Their contrasting indifference to slavery made many of their critics wonder whether they were not more devoted to Irish freedom than to liberty in America. Their continual devotion to Irish nationalism led to widespread purchases during the twentieth century of the bonds of a free Irish Republic which existed at the time only in the minds of its Sinn Fein exponents. Yet, however nationality-conscious, the Irish-Americans were not content to labor only for minority interests. Controlling the party politics of various metropolitan areas, they needed no inferiority complex to explain their devotion to the local Democratic machines. As generations passed, the "old sod" had only a romantic claim to interest, as against their increasingly practical devotion to the New World home.

Conservative and reactionary forces, however, anxious to maintain existing ways and institutions, and ofttimes their vested interests therein, were prompt to scent a danger on the horizon. Washington had expressed concern only about immigrants settling "in a body" and retaining their "languages, habits and principles (good or bad)." "Whereas," he added, "by an admixture with our people, they, or their descendents get assimilated to our customs, measures and laws:—in a word, soon become one people."[13] Jefferson, as well as Adams, questioned the wisdom of undue encouragement of immigration, lest Old World political influences or unbridled license be turned loose in the country.[14]

By the 1830's an organized nativism appeared in the chief seaports of the nation, which with patriotic appeal swelled into a movement which in the fifties depicted the menace of immigration and Catholicism as the real issue in American politics. The story of this quixotic crusade to protect the nation from foreigners and foreign influence is too long and has been too

[13] Worthington C. Ford, ed., *The Writings of George Washington* (New York, 1891), XII, 490.

[14] Andrew Lipscomb, ed., *The Writings of Thomas Jefferson* (Washington, 1903), II, 120; Charles F. Adams, ed., *The Works of John Adams* (Boston, 1850-56), IX, 584.

well told to need more than mention here.[15] Reiterating their challenge to substantial evils induced by the uncontrolled immigration of the time, the protagonists of this early brand of professional patriotism made their secret oath-bound order, generally labeled as the Know-Nothing Party, the stronghold of religious and political bigotry. Yet there is little evidence that the foreign-born, certain of their welcome in the Democratic party and—in the long run—in the nation, were thereby aroused to any great zeal to voice their consciousness of alien status in any aggressive way. This same factor offered them reassurance against later nativistic outbursts, including the Ku Klux Klan of the 1920's, although by that time new elements in the national picture and in the international scene were probably creating a sense of a minorities problem relating to foreign stocks in the United States.

While the peopling of America was achieved largely by the voluntary motivation of foreign immigration, it must be recognized that certain elements were added by a process of sudden and arbitrary transfer to a new jurisdiction. In such a case the expression, "minority nationality group," would seem to be more than a convenient sociological or anthropological classification.

The status of the Dutch in New York after the British conquest furnishes an interesting example of the treatment accorded to such a group. Under the English claim, New Netherland was part of the British royal domain even prior to its occupation after a show of force. The conquest followed a royal grant by charter to the Duke of York of proprietary rights with despotic "power and Authority of Government and Command in or over the Inhabitants of the said Territories or Islands."[16] Under this charter the Dutch population, technically intruders, could claim no such thing as rights.

In practice, however, Colonel Richard Nicholls, the deputy governor commissioned to achieve the subjugation of New Netherland, found it necessary to make numerous concessions that did not square with legal theory. His prudence and genius for conciliation were promptly evidenced in the articles of

[15] Ray A. Billington, *The Protestant Crusade, 1800-1860* (New York, 1938).

[16] This power was so unlimited as to be characterized by Professor Charles M. Andrews as "the most extreme expression of proprietary authority to be found in any of the feudal grants of soil and government in English America." See his *The Colonial Period of American History*, III (New Haven, 1937), 97.

capitulation under which the Dutch settlers were accorded definite rights.[17]

These terms of surrender, surprisingly favorable to the vanquished in continuing the Dutch system of law and local government, were confirmed in a proclamation issued by Governor Nicholls and in a code of laws, familiarly known as "The Duke's Laws," which he compiled, transferring to New York a composite of the legal institutions of the earlier English colonies, but with various Dutch features allowed to continue in the Dutch settlements. The Dutch type of central government was continued for twenty years without the usual English accompaniment of a representative assembly; the Dutch system of double or triple nomination and of partial retirement was used in local government; and other Dutch institutions, such as their system of land tenure upon the patroon estates, were maintained under the new jurisdiction.[18]

It was especially significant that the Dutch courts of New York City and of various Hudson River towns continued to function with Dutch magistrates chosen by Dutch inhabitants, administering Dutch law by Dutch methods in the Dutch language. Even after the English officials claimed that the reconquest of New Netherland in 1674 nullified the liberal provisions of the articles of surrender in 1664, Dutch judicial practices and influence continued to persist until finally superseded by more drastic judicial reorganization in the 1690's. Only as the number of English settlers increased did the operation of English law become a reality.[19]

The conquerors were also slow to impose their social institutions upon the Dutch population. The Duke's Laws of 1665 allowed the majority of householders in each parish to determine their own ecclesiastical allegiance; and Dutch churches, ministers, and schools increased during most of the colonial period. For some time not only did French Huguenots and the newly-arriving German element swell the membership of

[17] E. B. O'Callaghan, *Documents Relative to the Colonial History of the State of New York* (Albany, 1853-1887), II, 250-253.

[18] Victor H. Palsits, "The Transition from Dutch to English Rule, 1664-1691," Alexander C. Flick, ed., *History of the State of New York*, II (New York, 1933), 81-86. See also Albert E. McKinley, "The Transition from Dutch to English Rule in New York," *American Historical Review*, VI (1901), 695, 724.

[19] Julius Goebel, "The Courts and the Law in Colonial New York," Flick, ed., *History of the State of New York*, III (1933), 14-17.

the Reformed Dutch Church, but English Calvinists found it expedient to join these congregations despite the language difference. Some of the latter labored to force the use of English but it was not until 1763 that preaching in the official language was introduced into the Dutch church in New York City, a step which heralded the introduction of English in the services of all the Dutch churches. In many ways the Dutch congregations were more free than their English brethren from the opposition of the government to dissenters.

Under the English occupation various of the Dutch schools continued as the official agencies of education. In New York City this was terminated by the restoration of 1674—following the Dutch reconquest—whereupon the local school became exclusively a church school. Elsewhere the issue was postponed; new Dutch schools even made their appearance in various Dutch villages. By the middle of the eighteenth century, with the younger generation of Dutch tending to leave both their church and their school, the language issue was becoming a serious matter; soon instruction was offered in both Dutch and English. School textbooks, as well as religious literature, were long supplied from printing presses in Holland. Newspapers appeared in the colony only with the decline in the use of the Dutch language. Ventures in the vernacular of the older generation did not promise to be profitable, wherefore not a single Dutch-language newspaper made its appearance.[20]

The original Dutch settlers of New Netherland had experienced only a limited amount of happiness and contentment under Dutch rule. In a spirit of liberalism their conquerors had sought to justify their incorporation into the British Empire by a lenient attitude toward them and their institutions. The Dutch settlers, essentially a practical-minded folk, were easily reconciled to a new jurisdiction which brought to them little real oppression. A slow process of acculturation was soon under way, which by the American Revolution had largely assimilated the Dutch stock of New York, leaving traces, to be sure, of their distinctive background and of colorful contributions to the life of the colony and of the later state. Certainly no major issue of their minority status remained to complicate the currents of local politics.

[20] Augustus H. Shearer, "The Church, the School, and the Press," Flick, ed., *History of the State of New York*, III, 47-83.

The new republic carved by revolution out of the heart of the British Empire could be no less generous toward freshly incorporated increments. The Louisiana Purchase Treaty of 1803 specifically provided that the inhabitants of the ceded territory "shall be incorporated in the Union . . . and admitted as soon as possible . . . to the enjoyment of all the rights, advantages, and immunities of citizens of the United States; and in the mean time they shall be maintained and protected in the free enjoyment of their liberty, property, and the Religion which they profess."[21]

The resident population of Louisiana, led by the proud French Creoles who represented the oldest traditions of the colony, naturally resented their transfer to the jurisdiction of the boisterous young republic; they feared that their language, their customs, and their system of civil law would be crushed by an Anglo-American civilization. For the time, the old stock vastly out-numbered the newcomers, an advantage that continued with a steady decline until the 1840's. Yet an American administration, which symbolized an external control and an outside jurisdiction, was set up under Governor William C. C. Claiborne. Claiborne made strenuous efforts at coöperation and conciliation and symbolized his good will toward the Creole element in successive matrimonial alliances with two of their daughters.[22]

Creole culture in Louisiana, therefore, was not at all submerged by the new ways that the Americans introduced. The westward advance of the latter in due time reduced the preponderance of Creoles—temporarily strengthened by accretions from the French and Spanish West Indies—and made for a slow acceptance of American manners by the more docile masses. But American leaders were the proud champions of Creole ideals, which they labored vigorously to preserve. When, in 1816, Claiborne retired from the gubernatorial office to represent Louisiana in the United States Senate, he was suc-

21 William M. Mallory, ed., *Treaties, Conventions, International Acts, Protocols, and Agreements between the United States and Other Powers* (Washington, 1910), I, 509.
22 Isaac J. Cox, "William C. C. Claiborne," *Dictionary of American Biography*, IV, 115-116; George W. Cable, *The Creoles of Louisiana* (New York, 1884), 140-146; Lewis W. Newton, "Creoles and Anglo-Americans in Old Louisiana—A Study in Cultural Conflicts," *Southwestern Social Science Quarterly*, XIV (1933-34), 31-48.

ceeded by Jacques Philippe Villeré, scion of Creole stock who in time was impelled to proclaim: "The Louisianian who retraces the condition of his country under a government of kings can never cease to bless the day when the great American confederation received him into its bosom."[23]

For long, says the historian of the Creoles, "it was easy for Louisianians to be Americans; but to let Americans be Louisianians!—there was the rub."[24] It need not be pointed out that here was another aspect of the minorities problem. By the 1840's, however, the new forces were in a numerical preponderance. In the state constitutional convention of 1845, the irrepressible Bernard Marigny was only one of many who announced the crisis in the local cultural conflict:

The Anglo-Saxon race have invaded everything. They have supremacy in both houses of the legislature. . . . I know that the Anglo-Saxon race are the most numerous and therefore the strongest. We are yet to learn whether they will abuse the possession of numerical force to overwhelm the Franco-American population.[25]

Time revealed what a force the Creoles continued to be in the politics and in the culture of the state. However much they came to be overwhelmed by newer elements, however much their blood was diluted by intermarriage, they have continued as a distinctive element in the life of New Orleans and of Louisiana, giving it a local color that is cherished far and wide.

In the same way, the Spanish in Florida and the former citizens of Mexico in the Southwest have furnished no insoluble minorities problem. The only irredentist proposal worth noting was the stupid suggestion of the German foreign secretary, Alfred Zimmerman, in 1917, that Mexico might be tempted into an alliance with Germany by promises including the restoration of the "lost territory" of Texas, New Mexico, and Arizona.

Various aspects of the American constitutional system have combined with the incidents of life in a rapidly growing republic to reduce the danger of an "ausländer" minorities problem. The American concept of citizenship by naturalization—

[23] George W. Cable, *The Creoles of Louisiana*, 217.
[24] *Ibid.*
[25] Lewis W. Newton, "Creoles and Anglo-Americans in Old Louisiana," *op. cit.*, 47.

with expatriation from previous allegiance—has opened the door of opportunity to immigrants on nearly an equal footing with native-born citizens. To this European governments might and did protest, but the zealous American diplomacy that eventually secured recognition of this new system in a succession of treaties was almost invariably wielded in behalf of expatriates who were glad to become American citizens. The right of the foreign-born to a share in American civil liberties guaranteeing individual and minority rights has been a further safeguard against a minorities problem.

In the face of more recent developments, however, it can scarcely be denied that in the vast American mixing-bowl, viewed historically, there lie the seeds of a minorities problem that may, on the one hand, terminate or qualify the tradition of a generous treatment of aliens and adopted citizens and, on the other, threaten the unity and stability of the nation. The lesson of the past would seem to point to the absurdity of any action along the one line unless forced by developments along the other. It remains to be seen whether forces in the American scene have lost their power to repel the dictates of a nationalism which would reach out from a totalitarian Europe with claims upon population groups which have seemingly cast their lot in with other Americans of whatever origin.

The Present Position of Minorities in the United States

By

LOUIS WIRTH, Ph.D.*

THE United States, perhaps more than any other country in the world, has come to be known as a nation whose essential character has been shaped by the diverse origin of its people; and yet, paradoxically, in the United States we are least inclined to give official recognition to the existence of minorities within our bounds. The problems arising out of the divergent racial, national, and cultural origins of our people take on distinctive features largely because it is part of our formal national heritage that all men are, in principle even if not in fact, born equal, or, more precisely, that all men ought to be treated as political equals although in fact they differ in talents.

WHAT IS A MINORITY PEOPLE?

The conception of minority peoples that is current today has acquired its unique meaning largely because of the nationalistic movements in Europe and in the European colonies shortly preceding the first World War. It was crystallized in certain sections of the peace treaties following that war, which, among other things, gave official recognition to certain groups within European nations as minorities, and transformed some former minorities into autonomous nations, often with dominance over other minorities within their boundaries.

When we use the term "minorities" we are not primarily interested in a numerical relationship. The concept of minority people, either here or in Europe, is not a statistical one. Indeed in some countries, such as in South Africa, the ethnic groups suffering from the deprivations inherent in minority status are numerically in the majority. Professor Donald Young, in a recent monograph on *Minority Peoples in the Depression,*

* Professor of Sociology, University of Chicago.

137

considers them as comprising "those population groups distinguished from the dominant element by differentiating biological features of racial origin or by alien cultural traits, or a combination of both."[1] Sad as I or some of you may feel about the recent past and immediate prospects of the Republicans in this country, and tempted as I am to discuss their fate in the years that lie ahead, they are not as yet a minority people, although the Republican party is at present the minority party in our national political arena, occupying the place of what in England would be called His Majesty's most loyal opposition. I prefer, rather, to confine my discussion of minority peoples in the United States to those who, because of racial or cultural differences, are treated as a people apart or regard themselves as aliens in the country in which they live, and are, by virtue of this fact, held in lower esteem and debarred from certain opportunities open to the dominant group.

It is with reference to such groups and their relations with the dominant group that the problems of what we call "race relations" arise. The existence of these problems calls attention to the fact that the society in question has not as yet been knit together by intermarriage, interbreeding, free communication, and social intercourse into a single ethnic community. Since such relationships usually imply that the minority groups generally occupy a lower status in the society, have circumscribed opportunities, and often are subjected to distinct handicaps, it is to be expected that the disadvantaged position of the minorities should, under appropriate circumstances, express itself in a corresponding body of attitudes and sentiments, involving a sense of inferiority and sometimes even of persecution. When these sentiments and attitudes become obvious, we may know that we are dealing with a self-conscious minority. It is out of such groups that nationalistic movements have emerged in many parts of the world.

What matters, then, about minorities, is not merely their objective position involving their exclusion from certain privileges enjoyed by others in the community, but the conception that they have of themselves and of others in the society in which they live but of which they are not wholly a part, and con-

[1] Donald Young, *Research Memorandum on Minority Peoples in the Depression*, Social Science Research Council Bulletin No. 31 (New York, 1937), p. 1.

versely, the attitude which others, especially the dominant group in society, hold toward them. In brief, a minority group is one which, whether or not it suffers from discrimination and exclusion, conceives itself as the object of such differential treatment and is regarded by others as such.

WHO ARE THE AMERICAN MINORITIES?

The development of the United States as a national entity may well be conceived of as an aspect of the expansion of Europe. From the beginning of our national existence the settlements of America have witnessed the struggles between contending races and peoples. The technologically superior Europeans subjugated the indigenous Indians, and though the former were numerically in the minority for a long time, they reduced the native population to a state of permanent subordination. To the Indian minority there was soon added the minority of the black man, imported as indentured servant or slave from Africa. Today this latter group is large enough numerically to constitute our great racial minority.

The open door policy, practised as long as we were a country of unworked and seemingly limitless resources, attracted to our shores great successive waves of European peasants and townsmen. They came here in part through forced and in part through voluntary mass migrations. With the disappearance of the frontier and the industrial maturation of the United States during the decade following the World War, this mass influx came to a halt, although it should not be overlooked that even earlier in the nineteenth and early twentieth centuries sporadic signs of reluctance to receive further accretions to our population from abroad were evident. In particular, it should be noted that the shift from the older northern and northwestern European stock to the southern and eastern European migrants was accompanied by an accentuated apprehension in certain sections of the dominant groups in America. Although of the same race, broadly speaking, as the earlier white settlers, the so-called newer immigrants were thought of more or less as a group apart by virtue of their different socioeconomic status and cultural heritage. The passage of the quota immigration laws, giving preference to the stocks representing the first settlers or earliest immigrants, marked a definite end to the America which had been the "haven of the oppressed masses" of all nations.

Another distinct ingredient of our population is represented by the Oriental wave of migration. Aside from our legislation forbidding the future importation of slaves through the Statute of 1807, this group was the first to cause decisive legal barriers to be thrown up. Except for the relatively negligible migration from our own territorial possessions to the mainland and an insignificant amount of illegal immigration, this influx has been completely halted. Numerically far more important than the Orientals but distinctly less recognized as a minority is the Mexican population in the United States, which for a long time has constituted a minority element, especially in our Southwestern states, but which during the period of industrial expansion following the War found its way to the Northern cities and the Northwestern agricultural areas as well.

There are wide differences between the various sections of the country in the incidence of distribution of these major racial and ethnic groups. The Indian, insofar as he retains a tribal organization, appears as a significant element in the total population only in limited portions of the West and especially the Southwest. The Negro, formerly confined largely to the South and especially the Southeastern portion of the United States, and while still found there to a disproportionate extent, has established himself in large colonies in the great cities of the North. The older European immigrants are widely dispersed in the urban and the rural sections throughout the country, although in some agricultural states and in some of our great cities their presence in large numbers still gives a distinct flavor to whole communities and sections. The newer European immigrants, coming at the time of the greatest industrial expansion, are overwhelmingly concentrated in the larger industrial cities and retain to a much greater degree the compactness of their ethnic communities. In some cases their colonies in the cities of the United States exceed their numbers in the largest cities of their respective mother countries. The Orientals, though relatively negligible in numbers, are an important part of the population in a few limited localities of the Pacific Coast. There has been enough freedom of movement within the country, however, to give every section some representation of virtually every racial and cultural group.

While the racial and nationality groups indicated above constitute the heart of the minority problem in the United States, they do not exhaust the category of minority peoples in the United States. Although religious differences were by no means a negligible factor even in the early history of the nation, they have continued to be, and in some instances have become increasingly, significant bases for the emergence of differential status and treatment and for the development of group consciousness and conflict. In the face of the numerical as well as economic, social, and political dominance of the Protestant groups, the Catholic population may be regarded, and in certain communities thinks of itself, as a distinct minority, especially since in some communities Catholicism is also associated with Irish, Italian, Polish, or certain other ethnic or national origin. Whereas the internal divisions and lack of cohesion of the Protestant denominations detract from their capacity to play the role of a dominant group effectively, the relative internal unity and concentration of settlement of the Catholic groups in the urban centers increase their capacity to act collectively and to develop an appropriate group consciousness. Not unlike the Catholics, the Jews have in their earliest settlements in the United States been subjected to differential treatment, a variable degree of isolation, and for a time at least to the deprivation of certain civic rights. Not only culturally and especially religiously, but also as a consequence of recurrent movements of intolerance, the Jews even more than the Catholics may be thought of as a people with minority status in the United States. There are, in addition, other religious sects which by virtue of their creeds, their cultural heritages, and occasionally their isolated communal life are thought of as peoples apart. Among them are the Quakers, the Mormons, the Mennonites, the Amish, and of late, by virtue of the zeal of local vigilantes and enterprising journalists, Jehovah's Witnesses. Unlike the Jews and the Catholics, however, these groups are not sufficiently widely dispersed and imposing in numbers to be anything more than local minorities.

Our picture of minority peoples in the United States would not be complete, however, without depicting the existence in our midst of a variety of cultural islands, inhabited by peoples who as the result of a unique set of historical circumstances have retained or acquired peculiar social characteristics and

cultural heritages which set them apart from the larger surrounding world. Our Southern Highlanders, the French Cana-
dians of New England, the "Cajins" of Louisiana, and the hill
peoples of the Ozarks are among the groups who possess a distinctive or possibly archaic culture and in consequence are not
free to share fully in the cultural opportunities and the social
contacts open to others. It may be noted, however, that the high
degree of isolation under which such groups lived has prevented
the emergence of a sense of discrimination among them.

There are, of course, other dimensions to the concept of
minority peoples which it would be desirable but manifestly
impossible to treat here. The Okies, dramatized in the *Grapes
of Wrath*, consisting of the sharecroppers and the dispossessed
agricultural migrants of the marginal land areas, are no
doubt such a group, especially in the eyes of those Californians
who saw and acquired possession of Paradise first. The Communists, especially when deprived of the privilege of appear-
ing on ballots, and other groups seeking a hearing for their
doctrines or their grievances, no doubt are inclined to think
of themselves as oppressed minorities. But since most of these
groups are identified with their respective minorities by virtue of a common economic or political fate or by voluntary
affiliation rather than by birth, race, or cultural heritage,
they may properly be exempted from the category of minority peoples. At worst, their status is not much more permanent and pitiable than that of a political party after having
lost three successive national elections.

TRENDS IN MINORITY STATUS

It is not inappropriate in surveying the minority problem
in the United States to indicate the proportions of the size
of each of the major groups with reference to the total population. As of 1930, out of our total population of nearly
123,000,000, 88.7 percent were white, 9.7 percent Negro, 1.2 percent Mexican, .3 percent Indian, slightly over .1 percent Japanese, and less than .1 percent each Chinese, Filipino, Hindu,
Korean, and others. The proportion of the population of the
United States that is Negro has continued to decline every
decade over a period of more than one hundred years, although
their redistribution incident to the northward industrial mi-

gration has created a Negro problem in areas which until recently did not know it. As might be expected, the proportion of our population consisting of native-born whites has been increasing until in 1930 it was 73.8 percent. Even more striking is the fact that the native white population that was native-born of native parentage amounted to 43.5 percent. The proportion of our population that is native-born is increasing, as is the proportion of native-born of native parentage. This indicates that with the relative cessation of immigration and with the progress of intermarriage between various sections of our people we are, from the standpoint of our national stock, becoming more self-sufficient and are being welded into a more homogeneous entity, at least as far as the preponderant element in our population is concerned.

At the beginning of this year there were, according to the Alien Registration Director, nearly four and three-quarter million non-citizens residing in the continental United States. Of the immigrants who were within our midst in 1930, nearly one-third came before 1900. If we may take the ceremony of naturalization as an index to the assimilation of peoples, it may be noted that over 60 percent of the foreign-born white population in 1930 was naturalized. The evidence indicates that subsequently an even greater interest in becoming American citizens was manifested by the aliens in this country. No doubt the rules for eligibility for various forms of public assistance in the depression period were a great factor in this demand for citizenship. It should be noted, however, that naturalization is almost entirely a function of the time which the group has spent in this country. While we do not have the figures for this country, comparable Canadian data show that while such groups as the Poles have a lower rate of naturalization than the Austrians, this difference is eliminated or even reversed if we take account of the years of residence in their country of adoption.

When we consider the potentialities of immigrant groups to crystallize into blocs, however, it should be noted that the immigrants from the Scandinavian countries, from Germany, England and Wales, the Netherlands, Belgium, Switzerland, and France are to a very much higher degree naturalized than the Poles, Hungarians, Jugoslavs, and Italians, for instance. The increasing frequency with which Slavic and Italian names appear on ballots for public office, especially in metropolitan communities, indicates the degree of political power which some of the more recent immigrant groups with large urban concentrations have achieved, or the degree to which they have acquired actual political equality.

The statistics on foreign-born white population by country of birth (1930) indicate that of the 13,366,407 in this category the largest number (1,790,429) came from Italy, the next largest number (1,608,814) came from Germany, with Poland (1,268,583) next, and Russia (1,153,628) fourth. That the totalitarian nations of Europe have substantial representation of their subjects or former subjects here is a fact worth emphasizing in the light of their extended conception of nationality. If to this group be added the descendants of these foreign-born residents, who presumably are at least in part subject to the ideologies of their respective mother countries, we get an impressive segment of our total population. Of our total foreign white stock of 38,727,593, more than one-sixth is German (6,873,103) and nearly one-eighth (4,546,877) is Italian. If we note further that the Italians have the highest percentage of any of the major immigrant groups unable to speak English (15.7 percent in 1930), we have further reason to fear their exclusive susceptibility to news and propaganda purveyed by their foreign language press, which in part has been subsidized by agencies of the mother country's government.

The reduction in our immigration from about 650,000 a year in 1900 to less than 150,000 has not only affected the proportion of the actual foreign element in our population but also its rate of increase. Progressively the number of children immigrants produce is declining, and the difference between the native and foreign stocks and between the native whites and the Negroes in this respect is shrinking.

The heavy immigration of the three decades preceding the World War produced a profound shift in the composition of the foreign-born population of the United States. Whereas in 1910 this population consisted of 44.5 percent "new immigrants" and 55.5 percent "old immigrants," by 1930 the position was reversed to 54.6 percent "new immigrants" and 45.4 percent "old." The same trend is apparent with reference to the children of immigrants. Whereas in 1910 the native whites of foreign or mixed parentage came to the extent of

81.7 percent from the "old immigrant" stock, by 1930 this percentage had declined to 59.2 percent. One need not share the
bigotry of certain racial enthusiasts who ascribe all of the
virtues of the human race to the old immigrants (i.e., themselves) and all the vices to the new to recognize that the recent
ties to the Old World deriving from blood relationships and
descent have shifted from the northern and northwestern to
the southern and southeastern countries of Europe.

This shift in the source of our more recent immigration
has been accompanied also by a corresponding shift in religious
affiliation of the American population. Of the total church
members of the nation, slightly over one-half are Protestants,
a little over one-third Roman Catholics, and less than one-
tenth Jews. In addition, one must take account of the almost
infinite variety of sects who, although differentiated from one
another by minor doctrinal divergencies, regard themselves
as chosen or oppressed peoples destined to live in closed communities insulated from an unbelieving world.

Another shift of considerable importance that has occurred
in recent decades is that from rural to predominantly urban
concentration of the immigrants and their offspring. With few
exceptions, it may be said that the earlier the time of arrival
of the immigrant group, the more likely it was to take advantage of the still available cheap land. By the time emigration from southern and eastern Europe got fully under way,
this land supply was largely exhausted, and America's industrial
expansion lured the immigrants to the cities. As the waves of
newer emigration from Europe increased, the pressure that
formerly produced emigration from northern and northwestern
Europe declined, due in part to an industrial expansion in that
part of Europe itself. The problems of economic maladjust-
ment, of housing, of the urban slum, of health, of education,
and of social order that take such an aggravated form in the
large urban communities affect the recent European immigrants and the Negroes to a very much greater extent than was
the case a few decades ago.

The history of the racial and ethnic migrations to the United
States is also a history of the succession of earlier groups by
later groups in occupations and in positions of power and influence. The newcomers generally must content themselves with
the least desirable places in the social and economic world.

As a new group of invaders succeeds the old, it pushes them upward and is in turn pushed upward by the groups that follow. This social, economic, and political mobility operated fairly smoothly and continuously as long as there was plenty of room at the top. The depression, however, has called attention to the fact that this process cannot continue indefinitely and that we are approaching a stable if not a closed society.

The foreign-born are to a larger extent than the natives concentrated in the unskilled occupations, and while the foreign-born exceed the natives slightly in their proportion of the semi-skilled, skilled, and managerial positions, they are far behind the natives in the clerical and professional groups. There are, of course, great regional variations in the occupational distribution of natives and foreigners, and the preponderance of the natives in the agricultural occupations significantly affects their distribution in the various classes of non-farm work. While the depression seems to have retarded the economic ascendancy of the immigrant, as of course it has also that of the natives, it is clear that the immigrant is no longer restricted to the least desirable and the unskilled jobs, and that he is approaching the condition of the native in his occupational status. Very recently, in the formulation of the national defense program, it has been found that in certain highly skilled occupations in essential defense industries some of the key, skilled jobs are virtually monopolized by certain groups whose national origin makes them suspect.

In the case of the Negro, who began to take the place of the European peasantry in the northern cities during the war and post-war period, the situation was essentially similar, except that it was complicated and aggravated by the greater visibility of the Negro's racial marks and the more rigid caste-like lines which separated him from the white world. The Negro, more rigorously than the immigrant, was denied the full opportunities of living where he pleased, of joining trade unions to protect himself in his job, and of sharing fully in the cultural opportunities of American life. He was, as the saying goes, "the first to be fired and the last to be hired"; and in the higher occupational brackets was confined by prejudice to the exercise of his talents among his own racial group. Herded as he was into a racial ghetto, which had only reluctantly been abandoned by the whites—sometimes not without violence—he was forced to live under conditions of extreme poverty; unfit housing; inferior health, educational, and communal facilities; restricted cultural opportunities; and an impenetrable barrier of occupational discrimination.

The newer, industrial unionism, beginning with the period of the NIRA and culminating in the CIO, has resulted in breaking down some of the racial and minority handicaps. Class-consciousness has been to some extent substituted for race-consciousness. The fear of losing his job, which at an earlier period made the Negro an unlikely prospect for union recruitment in those rare instances where he was welcomed, has been abated somewhat by the protection extended through the National Labor Relations Act. Even the white worker, especially in the mass industries, has begun to see the necessity of organizing Negro labor in order to protect the gains achieved by labor generally. It remains true, however, that Negro trade union organization is still largely confined to the lower skilled occupations and to those where no monopolistic white trade union existed previously. While the Negro has been developing a middle class, consisting of civil servants, business men, and professional groups, even this élite has not been able to break through the racial walls which still effectually exclude the Negro from full participation in and recognition by the white world.

If there is any dominant trend in the race relations between the whites and the Negroes in the United States, it consists in the shift from a caste-like relationship to a class relationship. Whatever we may think about the desirability or undesirability of a class-structured society, it can at least be said that the latter offers more hope for eventual equality of opportunity on the basis of individual merit. While the status of a person as a member of a minority is ascribed to him on the basis of attributes over which he has no control, the dominant ideology of America still is to confer status on the basis of earned, as distinguished from inherited or categorically ascribed, characteristics.

FACTORS CONDITIONING MINORITY STATUS

The continued subordination over a long period of time of any special class in the population, when coupled with the concentration of that group in large numbers, with social visibility based on racial traits or cultural characteristics, with intense competition with the dominant group, and with rising levels of education, generally results in the emergence of group-consciousness and eventually of the overt struggle for recognition. In the case of the Negro we see that these factors, coupled with the disillusionment which he experienced after his unstinting contribution to our efforts in the first World War, has resulted in heightened race-consciousness and the emergence of racialist movements with militant ideologies, such as the Garvey movement. The resurgence of anti-Semitism in Europe appears to have furthered the group-consciousness of the Jews, and has even aided the revival of Jewish nationalism in the form of Zionism.

America has long been the country from which the renascent minorities of Europe have drawn sustenance, especially among the immigrants that they have sent to these shores. It may in truth be said, that the Americans of Irish descent and the Polish and Czechoslovakian colonies in the United States are, perhaps, more directly responsible for the achievement of national sovereignty of their respective minorities in Europe than their European compatriots themselves. Conversely, the loss of independence of some of these nations in the course of recent conquests is felt almost as deeply here among their erstwhile countrymen as it is by the conquered peoples themselves.

It is one of the characteristics of a dominant group that it seldom is aware of the minute differentiations within the subordinate groups. There is a general disposition on the part of the whites to deal with the Negro as an undifferentiated category. All Negroes are supposed to be alike, as are all Orientals, Jews, Catholics, Italians, and Germans. As a result, we carry around in our heads pictures or stereotypes which impute to each of these groups traits with reference to which they may be as highly differentiated as the dominant group. We have only recently learned that there is as much difference in intelligence, in criminality, and in other respects between Negroes as there is between whites, depending upon the situation in which the individuals find themselves. Such facts, however, are obscured by the minority status of these peoples, which limits their opportunities and affects the degree of discrimination with which they are treated as a group. If Negroes, as seems to be the case, have had a larger proportion of their members on relief, this is to be interpreted in the light not of their individual ability or willingness to work, but rather of the glaring discrimination in economic opportunities to which they are consigned. Not all Germans in this country are Nazis, not all Italians Fascists, nor all Russians Communists, just as not all Americans are New Dealers, nor all Negroes Republicans.

The more ample the group's opportunities have been to blend with the rest of the population, through marriage, social intercourse, and economic, political, and cultural life, the more like the dominant group in America do they become, the greater the difference will be between the individual members of the group, and the less will they represent the stereotype which we have been carrying around in our heads. Since minorities depend for their continued, separate existence upon distinguishable racial marks or culturally visible traits, it is clear that intermarriage and increasing equality in social intercourse will in the course of time undermine their separate identity. That this has actually been taking place in the United States is evident not merely in the case of the European immigrants but of the Negro and the Indian as well.

Since the first World War, and especially since the rise of the totalitarian states of Europe, a new factor has appeared upon the scene which profoundly influences the status of minorities in the United States. With the drying up of the streams of immigration from Europe, we were well on the way to the elimination of the minority problems of the European immigrants. These problems had actually reached a point where students saw little left to explore and where we were about ready to turn the matter over to the historians to put the archives in order. Organizations concerned with the problem of the immigrant were beginning to suffer from lack of support, because the philanthropic public could only with difficulty be persuaded that the problems of Americanization were serious enough to merit special attention. Even the settlement houses, traditionally concerned with the adjustment of the immigrant, were looking for other worlds to conquer. There was still, to be sure, some little interest in the immigrant; there was the romantic interest in the quaint and exotic, there was the moralistic interest in the alleged immigrant criminality, there was the humanitarian interest in his poverty, and there was the ritualistic interest in his citizenship, coupled with the fear that he was more susceptible to revolutionary doctrine and that he might actually claim the full rights of citizenship. But in trade and commerce, in the field of labor and in the professions, in education, religion, and politics the immigrant was sloughing off his minority status. This was by no means true, of course, of the Negro; for despite the multiplication of the mulatto the Negro remained a visible being apart, and his inferior status was fortified by the perpetuation of the life of great numbers of his race in the South, where deep historical traditions impeded his upward mobility. But even in the case of the Negro, lynchings declined and a semblance of educational equality of opportunity was opened to him. In some cases he even became a factor in politics, and in many avenues, particularly in the arts, he received outstanding recognition.

The depression, by inhibiting the possibilities of economic rise, also retarded the individuation which had gone on in the past. Only in a few cases, and rarely at that, did any of the minority groups prefer the static but cramped position behind their own ethnic walls, isolated from the streams of American life. Whereas formerly in the Americanization movement an enlightened policy dictated that the immigrant should not break too rapidly with his old world culture and sever his loyalties to the mother country too abruptly, today we are reminded (by the ardent wooing of immigrants by the governments of their mother countries) that the continuance of this former policy of ours may seriously undermine our national solidarity. Ingenious and well-financed Nazi agencies have been set up to tie the Germans abroad to the mother country. This includes not merely the immigrants themselves but their descendants as well. The distinctive tactics of these agencies have been to appeal to the bonds of blood relationship, to the virtually total neglect of cultural ties which earlier were considered dominant.

To be sure, many representatives of the population of the totalitarian states are deeply humiliated and sincerely apologetic for what their respective Old World governments do. Many of them are in open alignment against the policies of these governments and are attempting to perpetuate some of the values inherent in the pre-dictatorial heritages of their respective mother countries. The number of those who stand in open antagonism to the doctrines and policies of the totalitarian states has been recently augmented somewhat by the numbers of refugees from these countries who have personally suffered from persecution. For many of these people America is not so much a land of golden opportunity as it was for their predecessors who came to these shores, but again a haven of refuge.

AMERICAN MINORITIES IN PROSPECT

The propaganda campaign which the dictatorial states have inaugurated goes farther than the attempt to revitalize or to generate loyalty to the country of origin on the part of the immigrant. It is designed not merely to develop, no matter on what artificial grounds, an oppression psychosis, but to create militant outposts for penetration and eventual conquest —peaceful or otherwise—of this country and of the world. That the dictatorial countries, especially the Nazis, are not unaware of the opportunities which our many unsolved minority problems furnish them is indicated by the following statement attributable to the Nazi propaganda minister:

Nothing will be easier than to produce a bloody revolution in America. No other country has so many social and racial tensions. We shall be able to play on many strings there. North America is a medley of races. The ferment goes on under cover of democracy, but it will not lead to a new form of freedom and leadership, but to a process of decay containing all of the disintegrating forces of Europe. The America of today will never again be a danger to us.[2]

Or, as the head of the Nazi government has put it:

Our strategy . . . is to destroy the enemy from within, to conquer him through himself. The place of artillery preparation for frontal attack by the infantry in trench warfare will in future be taken by revolutionary propaganda, to break down the enemy psychologically before the armies begin to function at all. The enemy people must be demoralized and ready to capitulate, driven into moral passivity, before military action can even be thought of. We shall not shrink from the plotting of revolutions. . . . We

[2] Hermann Rauschning, *The Voice of Destruction* (New York: G. P. Putnam's Sons, 1940), p. 71.

shall have friends who will help us in all the enemy countries. We shall know how to obtain such friends. Mental confusion, contradiction of feeling, indecisiveness, panic: these are our weapons.

The German component of the American people will be the source of its political and mental resurrection. The American people is not yet a nation in the ethnographical sense; it is a conglomerate of disparate elements. But it is the raw material of a nation. . . . We shall soon have an S. A. [storm troops] in America. We shall train our youth. . . . Into the hands of our youth will be given the great statesmanlike mission of Washington which this corrupt democracy has trodden under foot.[3]

Direct utterances in a similar vein by these and other spokesmen for totalitarianism are available in abundance. That these are not idle words is indicated by the happenings in such countries as Czechoslovakia, Poland, Denmark and Norway, Holland, Belgium, and France. New organizations for this purpose, such as the German-American Bund, have been organized, and old ones whose loyalty to America once was beyond doubt have been converted into open or unwitting arms of the Nazi propaganda ministry. A similar situation, though not so effectively organized, prevails in the case of Italian fascism. Although our foreign language press had been declining markedly, certain papers have been given a new lease on life through their rediscovery as propaganda media by the Nazi and Fascist governments.

One of the chief weapons employed in the penetration of foreign countries by the Nazis is the ideology of race. Largely as the result of concerted propaganda, and recently of war, the racial myth has become an instrument of political revolution. One question which America will therefore have to face is the question of whether the Nazi doctrine of racism is likely to make progress in the United States. At first glance one would think that in a country so diverse in its ethnic and racial composition as ours the prospect of infection by the virus of racism is negligible. But we should not underestimate the latent feelings of racial prejudice and the racial and ethnic conflicts which, given adverse economic circumstances, war, and propaganda, can be roused to white heat.

There have, of course, been organizations based on racial and religious intolerance in the United States for a long time.

[3] *Ibid.*, pp. 8-10; 70.

Anti-alien, anti-Negro, anti-Oriental, anti-Catholic, and anti-Semitic movements have risen and declined as our internal social and economic problems have become more acute and in turn subsided. Experience, not merely of this country but elsewhere, indicates that the appeal of intolerance movements is not very great in periods of general prosperity. Let the struggle for existence and for status among substantial parts of the population become intense, and let the winds of adversity sweep over great sections of the nation, and the stage is set for the acceptance of the preachment of racial hate. Those who have lagged in the climb to fortune, prestige, and power become susceptible to propaganda which assures them that they belong to the superior race, reminds them that they were here first, and convinces them that they have been cheated out of their birthright by the cunning of an inferior group of late-comers, who must again be pushed back into their place and stripped of the advantages they have so unfairly acquired.

The usual formula of such movements is to lay the blame for your insecurity, your unhappiness and frustrations, on the mischief of an alien or minority group, thus providing yourself at one and the same time with a scapegoat to bear the burden of your own inadequacy and a means for expanding your ego. It is a pathetic but interesting fact that those who pride themselves on their race—with which, of course, they have had nothing whatsoever to do—generally have little else to be proud of. It was not until a considerable stratum of the southern Negroes had already outstripped the "poor whites" that the prejudice against the black man became virulent. As some of the immigrant groups have moved upward in the socio-economic scale, the full fury of nativism and know-nothingism and anti-alien movements became evident. It was the energetic Japanese rather than the allegedly more placid Chinese that furnished the keenest competition and became the objects of the bitterest discrimination to the whites on the Pacific Coast. Wherever and whenever there is a noticeable contraction of economic opportunity, restriction of social mobility, loss of security, and accentuation of competition, we may also expect the latent antagonisms between dominant and minority groups to become overt and the lines separating them to harden. This fact has been driven home to us by the depression of the decade just closed.

It has frequently been charged by clever but unscrupulous propagandists from the totalitarian states, that our professed sympathy for the persecuted racial, ethnic, and religious minorities of Europe rested upon nothing more than transparent hypocrisy. They have tried to contrast our practice with our professed policy. But it should be noted that *they* have adopted the persecution of racial, religious, and political minorities as a part of their official national policy, and have sought to rationalize this policy and to silence our protests by reminding us that the most enlightened democracy, namely ours, is guilty of the same practice. We are in a position to reply, however, that whatever may be the disabilities from which certain sections of our population suffer by virtue of their racial, religious, or ethnic affiliations, this discrimination is only in exceptional cases a matter of our national laws or countenanced as a matter of public policy. In large measure it is an archaic heritage from a past which we are attempting to outlive, and promising and strenuous efforts are under way toward its complete elimination. We can say finally with a perfectly clear conscience, that whereas the Nazi régime suppresses with brutal terror any challenge to its racial doctrines and persecution, in our case the opportunity to carry on open counter-agitation against such doctrines and discrimination remains an inviolate civic right.

I would not minimize the severe legal and customary handicaps from which the Negro, the Indian, and the Oriental suffer. Deprivation of the franchise, restrictions of the rights of citizenship, unequal treatment under the law, discrimination in public employment and public conveyances, deliberate segregation and Jim-Crowism, unequal educational opportunities— all these and many more are by no means mythical. Beyond the realm of legal and official inequalities there is the even wider range of the cramping effect of prejudice and exclusion. These are realities that cannot be lightly glossed over; nor can we condone, although in the hysteria of world disorder and threatening war we can understand, much of the irrational and unnecessary attempts to enact anti-alien legislation, such as that which singles out the alien alone for fingerprinting. These, however, are matters which time and a recovery of a measure of sanity in the world will probably to a large extent remedy. At any rate, the direction of our national policy with reference to these matters is clear, as is the dominant trend of public sentiment.

One reason why we have been so relatively free from violent conflict between the dominant and the minority groups, and why we can hope to be even freer from it in the future, is to be found in our constitutional provisions and our Bill of Rights, which commit us to a policy of toleration or laissez-faire in the realm of cultural life, to the absence of a state religion, and to at least the formal declaration of the equality of men before the law. Our recent policy toward our territorial out-posts again lends strength to the belief that we can resist the ideologies of racism and of world imperialism. The support which the efforts to reduce lynchings have received from the South itself is another encouraging sign. The recent efforts on the part of our government to make good as far as we can some of the grave injustices to the Indian minority, by putting into effect a policy far more humane than any we have ever attempted before, including the effort to preserve as much as possible of their cultural heritage and their cultural au-tonomy, are another encouraging sign of enlightenment. Whereas the totalitarian countries are suppressing their minori-ties at home and are busy trying to turn their former nationals into fifth columns abroad, we are, after all, making some determined efforts to minimize the adverse effects of minority status, if not to eliminate minorities altogether—not by ex-tirpation but by keeping open the door of uncoerced assimila-tion. Unfortunately, precisely at the time when we are most concerned about assimilating the alien in our midst as speedily as possible, our hope to achieve this end is marred by the suspicion with which, in time of stress, we regard every im-migrant and every person of alien cultural heritage. Whether our efforts toward national preparedness will serve as a suffi-ciently powerful solvent of racial, ethnic, and cultural differ-ences to counteract the tendency toward witch-hunting, which such a crisis is likely to generate, is highly problematical.

It is not to be hoped that in the face of the totalitarian onslaught our attitude of toleration of differences, our cultiva-tion of cultural pluralism, and our recently-gained awareness of the discrepancy between our legal and ethical standards on the one hand and our actual practices on the other, will con-tinue uninterruptedly. Just as, at an earlier period in our history, we had the difficult problem of conscience, of reconciling the perpetuation of slavery with the spirit of the Declaration of Independence and the Constitution, so today we face the task of reconciling our genuine concern about national unity and defense with the toleration of variant and often segregated and alien modes of life among our national minorities.

The future of the status of our minorities will, of course, necessarily depend in part upon the outcome of the present war, and upon the peace and the new world order that will eventually follow. But it will depend also, in large measure, upon an official and unofficial domestic policy which will operate consistently in every sphere to bring our collective conduct as a nation and our private lives as citizens more closely into accord with our professed ideals of a democratic order.

Can Minorities Be Tolerated in a Democracy?

By

CARL KELSEY, Ph.D.*

EVERY thinking man knows the importance and difficulty of this subject. Our ideals, stated theoretically, may not vary widely, but our opinions as to the best ways of realizing our ideals are strangely divergent. Luckily, or unluckily, social programs have not been based on the ideas or knowledge of experts, real or alleged. In every day life people act to meet needs and satisfy emotional drives, then reflect and rationalize. For instance, I do not believe that there is evidence that the human races can be classified on a basis of ability. I know no correlation between physical traits and ability. This is not the popular attitude anywhere on earth. Hitler is much more confident of a pure German race than are the German anthropologists. The Japanese, headed by the "Son of Heaven" are equally sure of their inherent superiority.

It is obvious that all the folks of earth are not on the same cultural level. The poor folks may envy the rich and claim that their poverty is due to lack of opportunity—not to their inferiority—but even then seldom do they desire the "way of life" of the others. The richer folks, on the contrary, are confident of their natural superiority. The Eskimo does not want to live like an Arabian nomad, nor like a factory worker here. The Arab sneers at our "way of life" as well as at our ideals. Not all people worship wealth, nor talk in terms of progress. This is the first basic fact to be kept in mind.

Here we find, perhaps, a clue to part of our present dilemma. Not long ago we had a "way of life." Modern discoveries and inventions have upset or made impossible that "way" for a large part of our population. The result is a confusion of ideals, an uncertainty, a doubt as to the worthwhileness of older

* Professor of Sociology, University of Pennsylvania.

policies. Once man was taught to "cast his burdens on the Lord." Now it is proclaimed that the state will look after him. Is the state likely to succeed where the Lord failed?

This brings us to another basic consideration. What is to be the ideal man is to seek? Are we to emphasize the development of individuals to the utmost, or shall we stress the smooth functioning of the human machine? The first is the base of philosophical anarchy; the second of communism. The first is caricatured in the school program of letting each child do only that which he desires. The second leads us to a way of life similar to that in a beehive, each member doing his assigned task. Anarchy leads to warfare and communism to stagnation. Here is the dilemma. Moreover, if we accept the second alternative, are men to be organized in local groups, racial perhaps in origin, on national lines, or on a world basis more comprehensive than man has ever dreamed? World empires have been sought, but not for the welfare of mankind. Are not millions of Europeans today but "hewers of wood and drawers of water" on behalf of a dominant group?

Not long ago man was a hunted, as well as a hunting animal. His numbers were small; his life, short and uncertain. Now man has spread over the earth, bringing destruction to other forms of life and changing the very surface of the earth, not always for the better. Now he faces the problem of getting enough from the earth to maintain himself. Remember that man "does not live by bread alone." Ignored in the main, the population problem lies behind most of the world situation today. I can but mention this fact and time does not permit even a statement of the various attitudes of students. Man must learn that size of population has a bearing on his standard of life as well as on his attitude toward other folks. Free commerce is almost unknown. Can the Du Ponts save us if Japan should stop our rubber imports? "In the international politics of this world, the truth is frail that ignores a mountain range or an ocean," writes Griswold in *Harper's* for August 1940.

Let me attempt a brief summary. We have to do with an actual organization, not with an idealized scheme. Actually we humans are organized locally in the main and we think in local terms rather than general. To be sure, we no longer think

wholly in terms of the family, clan, or tribe, but, in most regards, our minds are limited by country or government.

Throughout history man has used but three forms of organization in all his institutions, so far as I can see. Do not forget
the word *all* even though the illustrations are from the state.
The names of the three forms are many. (1) All men are equal—
in theory of course. Call it democracy. (2) Delegated government such as our constitution sought to provide. (3) Despotism,
with power from above. All forms have their merits and defects. I quote from Leviathan,[1] a recent and very thoughtful
analysis which merits attention. The author, R. M. MacIver,
says that we must distinguish between

the form of *government* and the form of the *state* itself. No form
of government is permanent, but there are abiding forms of the
state. Democracy is such a form and wherever it has existed in the
past or exists in the present, it can be identified by two simple
criteria. . . . The two are as follows: (1) Democracy puts into effect the distinction between the state and the community. . . .
(2) Democracy depends on the free operation of conflicting opinions.

The trend away from democracy has been vividly described
by Herbert Hoover.

Excluding Russia, which really never enjoyed any system of liberty, and Spain, where democracy was overthrown in the clash between communists and fascists, 250,000,000 people have almost
bloodlessly surrendered all guarantees of personal liberty. For years
previously the nations in this group had, by the tests of free speech,
free press, free public meetings, and of trial by jury, enjoyed most
of the spiritual and intellectual liberties. They had won these rights
by bitter struggle over two centuries. In all these countries the
economic systems had long been much the same as ours. They were
based on the right of men to choose their own callings; to acquire
and retain private property for the security of their families and
old age. They were systems of free private enterprise.[2]

As to the cause of the change Mr. Hoover found that

the first outstanding fact was that the stupendous revolution in
ideas and government in these many nations had been made at
the will of the people themselves. . . . Liberty committed suicide.
The universal pattern was that in every country the people had

[1] R. M. MacIver, *Leviathan,* Louisiana State University Press, 1939.
[2] *American Mercury,* July 1940.

despaired that democracy could solve their economic and governmental problems.[3]

It must be that folks have forgotten, or no longer believe, the old lines of Pope,

> Of all the ills that men endure
> How small the part that laws
> Can cause or cure.

Even the casual observer must note the steady growth of executive, bureaucratic power in our own government despite the provisions of the constitution. No one fails to see the steady increase of state control over our personal activities in the fields of industry, health, and education, nor do we forget the extension of national control as compared to local or state functions.

This centralization is not limited to our political organization. Trade unions began as educational agencies, but now they seem to carry out the injunction to go "into the highways and hedges and compel them to come in." John Lewis in his rise to power is said to have used methods which would have done credit to Diaz. Democratically controlled religious groups are generally small and torn by inner conflicts quite in contrast to the Roman Catholic Church. Hitler would control the church, and Japan has practically ordered all foreign missionaries to leave, while their properties, educational or religious, are to be put in the hands of Japanese who will do as the government desires.

We must stop, very briefly, to ask the merits and defects of this centralized control as over against our older democratic ways. The great weakness of democracy is revealed, perhaps, in the old quip; "The fish swims; the snake crawls; the dog runs; man is the only animal that talks himself forward." MacIver, in the book already mentioned, states the vitally weak spot in the other plan. "Every alternative to democracy is subject to a charge more fatal than any that can be laid against it, the memorable defect of irresponsible power."[4]

Many years ago Bentley, in his book, *The Process of Government*, a work which never received the attention it merited,

---

[3] Summary in *Reader's Digest*, September 1940.
[4] *Leviathan*, p. 89.

pointed out that no one man could be the embodiment of a great people—the "hundred percent American," to use a current term. Each individual belongs to some, or many, smaller groups, whether racial, economic, religious, or geographical. That which seems to help his group comes to be extolled as wise national policy. Thus government must be the result of a compromise between various (and changing) interest groups. Marx, in his "class conflict" theory oversimplified the situation and developed a messianic concept which made the employers the enemies of society, the working class its saviors. Bentley also pointed out that not all groups were of the same nature. He drew a line between interest and discussion groups. Here we are holding a meeting of a discussion group. We are free to take any position we desire, say what we please or fail to pass a resolution, even. The phrase "there ought to be a law" has long been a standing joke. Actual government, however, is not run by discussion groups, by the "ought-to-be's," and, in passing, let us note that with every expansion of governmental function the power of bureaucracy grows. If we but assume that the men in office are sincere in their belief that they are needed in their positions, their power in election times when the government is spending money lavishly can be surmised.

In no large country—regardless of the form of government —have all citizens equal weight. This is true in all social institutions, even in the smaller ones like the family. Many folks have little influence, some few have great influence. In the large democratic aggregates the difficulty of picking leaders wisely grows apace, whereas in small groups the qualifications of a given man for a given place are easily known. It is doubtful if the radio has helped in this matter.

Democracy, then, puts the responsibility on the individual. He may, and does, make endless mistakes, but as a rule they affect but few persons. No one else has to follow his example or do as he says, nor do others control him. The result is what we are pleased to call "liberty" or "freedom."

By contrast, in the centralized scheme, a few decide, the rest obey, and the effects of a bad decision are shared by all, the young pigs being killed, perhaps. But a wise decision may benefit all. This is not the main issue. The real problem grows out of the carefully cultivated fiction that the governors are supermen who know best. The answer to this was well written in 1879 by a life-long democrat, William Graham Sumner.[5]

It is called the state, and all kinds of poetical and fanciful attributes are assigned to it. It is presented, of course, as a superior power, able and ready to get us out of trouble. . . . When, however, all the fine phrases are stripped away, it appears that the state is only a group of men with human interests, passions, and desires, or, worse yet, the state is, as somebody has said, only an obscure clerk hidden in some corner of a governmental bureau. In either case the assumption of superhuman wisdom and virtue is proved false. The state is only a part of the organization of society in and for itself. . . . The task of society, however, has always been and is yet, to secure this organization, and yet to prevent the man in whose hands public power must at last be lodged from using it to plunder the governed,—that is, to destroy liberty.

Speaking for myself, I challenge the growing belief that the best interests of men in the future are to be met by becoming slaves of the state. I seem to hear Sumner's voice saying, as he did, that when that time came the thing to do was to get on the central committee. I see no reason to think that state slavery will prove more endurable than the older slavery.

If we knew more in detail what has happened in Germany and Italy I think we should find that the men driven out or "concentrated" were those of great ability, not little. I think too that we should find plenty of self-exaltation and grasping for personal power. In a word, no change in the mere form of government will really solve our problems. I am reminded of the wise comment of William Penn in the preface to his *Frame of Government.*

When all is said, there is hardly any frame of government so ill designed by its first founders that in good hands would not do well enough; and story tells us the best, in ill hands, can do nothing that is great or good. . . . Governments, like clocks, go from the motion men give them; and as governments are made and moved by men, so by them they are ruined too. Wherefore governments rather depend on men than men on governments.

I admit, freely, that democracy grows more difficult as the population increases. I suspect that what we really want is centralized administration, not centralized with policies decided by divine or diabolical inspiration.

[5] *The Forgotten Man.*

Let us now turn to consider the situation of certain minority groups in this country. Our national policies have not been uniform, nor consistent. Some small groups, isolated, like the Alaskan Eskimo, have been almost completely ignored. Long ago we adopted a reservation policy for the Indians, moving many by force to new locations. One is reminded at once that the present real or proposed forced migrations in Europe involving millions of persons are really a new experiment so foreign to our beliefs that we may omit further mention of them. We should not forget, however, the early proposals to move the Negro to Liberia or Mexico. Here, in the main, there has been no forced geographical segregation of different groups. Some small groups of kindred folks whose ethical ideals corresponded to those of the others such as the Homestead and Amana communistic settlements met little hostility and aroused considerable interest. Nevertheless a counterpart of the caste system has developed in our attitude toward the Negro. The Negroes live on reservations with social, not geographical, boundaries, but the limits are both uncertain and changing. We must, nevertheless, treat race prejudice as a fact and not expect sudden and drastic changes.

Since the level of Negro development has been lower than that of the whites it has been easier for the ambitious Negro boy or girl to get ahead of his group. It has been suggested that the Negro should train his professional men—lawyers, doctors, teachers and others—with their practice limited to Negroes. At times such a program might work well but would break down completely in isolated regions. Moreover, it has been hard to develop confidence in their own men among the Negroes themselves, particularly where high technical skill is involved. We must recall that medical fakirs are not wholly idle in the white groups. Separate schools are simple where hundreds of children are involved, but become impossible where a handful of Negroes are surrounded by thousands of white children. Yet one is blind who does not see that the present influx of Negroes into the Philadelphia high schools causes some serious problems. Time and infinite patience will be required to work out the most satisfactory adjustment for all these questions. To limit the development of an individual, to set bounds to his achievements because of membership in some given group is both depressing and dangerous, but this is just what race prejudice does. Moreover, it stimulates the building of defense mechanisms which do not aid in solving the difficulties. I know, therefore, no final solutions.

There seem to be two widely different concepts in our ideas as to social progress. One man thinks to find some permanent policy which will eliminate the troubles. To my mind social problems grow in complexity in every civilization as larger and larger numbers are involved. We cannot go back if we would. Henceforth this country is involved in world affairs from which we cannot isolate ourselves. The Indian is caught in a white man's culture. He cannot save himself by remaining an Indian and maintaining a distinct culture. We face, therefore, an eternal problem of finding new solutions under changed conditions for what are, after all, hoary questions. Man does not change, but the conditions under which he lives do—and for these changes man himself is largely responsible. There are differences between whites and blacks, but they have many more things in common and the latter seem to me the more important. Where shall we put the emphasis? Condemnation of past policies will get us nowhere. Old shibboleths are useless. I know of no difference between Democrats and Republicans on international relations. Rather than despair, we must tackle our problems hoping that we may work out new "ways of life" as did our ancestors. Destruction is easy, but not necessary. My own attitude is well stated by Edwin Markham in his poem "Man-Making":

> We are all blind until we see
> That, in the human plan,
> Nothing is worth the making if
> It does not make the man;
> Why build these cities glorious
> If man unbuilded goes?
> In vain we build the world unless
> The builder also grows.

Consequences of Mass Immigration

By

ALVIN S. JOHNSON, Ph.D.*

Ours is a period of vast migrations. Not since the breakdown of the Roman Empire, and the southward drift of the Germanic tribes has there been such a wholesale uprooting of peoples as the flight of the Jews from Russia after Kishinev, the "exchange of populations" between Turkey and Greece after the World War, the forcible return to Germany of the German communities of Latvia, Estonia, Lithuania, the Ukraine, Bessarabia, and the even more ruthless expulsion of Rumanians from German and Hungarian territory, of the Poles from Western to Central Poland and of Jews from Austria and Germany and their flight to every quarter of the world. Before the uneasy continent of Europe becomes stabilized once more we must expect even more extensive migrations of peoples thrust out by the conquerors or seeking escape from tyranny.

To the receiving country there are wide differences between the various types of immigration, differences that do not turn on quantity alone. In the second half of the nineteenth century enormous numbers of Irish, Germans, Scandinavians, Poles, Czechs, Italians, Russian Jews immigrated into America. With the exception of the first wave of Irish immigrants, of the small but important immigration of liberal Germans in 1848, and of the Jews from Russia, American immigration from 1850 to the World War was dominated by the individualistic impulse of economic self betterment. Prevailingly the people who came to us from Europe were of the poorer classes, laborers or peasants seeking higher wages and free or cheap land. They were the people who did most of the heavy work of building our railroads, of opening our mines, of exploiting our forests. They played an important role in breaking our Western prairies, in building our cities. Among the immigrants there was, to be sure, a considerable contingent of skilled mechanics who were

* Director, New School for Social Research, New York City.

of great importance to our developing industry. But by and large the effect of our pre-World War immigration was to oust the older American from the unskilled employments and to open up for him a wide range of skilled, semi-professional and business employments.

How the ethnic differences between the mass of common labor, on the one hand, and the skilled, professional, and business classes on the other, affected our social economic structure, our business practices, our politics and ideals is an inquiry that would take us too far afield. The essential fact is that in spite of the great mass of immigration, the older Americans continued to control our economic development. It was the older Ameri can who ran ahead of settlement and opened up the newer regions. It was he who fixed our lines of transportation. Our habits of consumption, our standards of living, our conception of education, our political ideals were set by the older Americans. The immigrants adapted themselves as promptly as possible to the ways of the natives. If this was seldom perfectly achieved by the immigrant himself, his children, nevertheless, became regular Americans, hardly distinguishable from the older stocks except by names of alien origin.

The world of today is more concerned with another type of mass immigration, the immigration originating not in attraction by superior opportunities, but in propulsion, extending not to the working class alone but to the entire range of employments, unskilled and skilled labor, the professions and business. This kind of immigration is nothing new in history. On the revocation of the French edict of tolerance, in 1685, hundreds of thousands of Huguenots were expelled from France. They represented every class, although the professional and business classes formed a larger proportion than they had formed in the general population. A hundred thousand of them settled in England. Many others fled to Switzerland, Rhineland Germany, the Low Countries, and a contingent found its way to America. The Puritans and Quakers represented a similar migration of all classes, as did the so-called Pennsylvania Dutch, really non-conforming Germans. I have mentioned the Russian Jewish immigration of the nineties and the first decade of this century. The Jewish immigration from Germany since the advent of Hitler includes all classes, again with an abnormal proportion of the business and professional classes. We may be certain that whatever immigration we may have after the present war will conform to this general type.

It is to be observed, first of all, that this type of mass immigration is more resistant to the forces of assimilation than the first type which I have described. When a whole race or religious faction, or the population of a whole province, is expelled from its native habitat, it necessarily brings along its business organizers, its intellectual leaders. These are by no means prepared to throw overboard all their own methods, their own standards and ideals, to put in their place unquestioningly those of the receiving country. The Huguenots in England remained essentially French, speaking the French language, following French ways of life, for the better part of a century. The tenacity of Puritanism in American life is proverbial. The Quakers have maintained their characteristics, and so, in large measure, have the Pennsylvania Germans. Contrast the New Amsterdam Dutch, who were drawn to America by the lure of business and employment. They have become completely merged in the general population. The Jews of the late immigration from Russia have exhibited no such tendency toward assimilation as the Jews who came with the Forty-Eighters. It may be said justly that the very fact of large numbers has had something to do with retarded assimilation. That is true, but only part of the truth. An immigrant group that has its own religious teachers, its own writers and journalists, its own business and professional men, is less under compulsion to conform to the ways of the native community than the unskilled workers scattered through the native population.

This is one side of the question. Instinctively we place a high value on assimilation. Very few Americans, to be sure, are so benighted as to yearn for homogeneity of blood, a condition that can obtain only in isolated communities, as among the Esquimaux—perhaps. But homogeneity of language, manners, living standards—in short, in externals—makes life run more smoothly.

But there is another side to be considered. The Huguenots in England did not simply place themselves at the disposal of existing English industry and business, as unskilled, or at best skilled laborers. They set up new industries. The British silk industry owes its origin to the Huguenots. So too a large section of the glass industry, leather working, furniture making, fine woollens, linens. Indeed, the industrial preeminence of England in the period leading up to the industrial revolution was largely the work of the Huguenots. In our own country the best agriculture down through the nineteenth century was that of the Pennsylvania Germans. In my native state of Nebraska a Pennsylvania German farm was expected to be a model of good tillage, an example to the neighborhood. What the "Forty-Eighter" Germans contributed to the organization of music and musical education is known to everybody. The Jews who are descended from the refugees from Russia have played an enormous part in the development of our musical and artistic life. It is hard to say what Hollywood would have been without them.

To those who believe that our American civilization has reached its limit, that our methods of business and industry are already established on the highest possible level, the only kind of immigrant who seems desirable is the one who takes his place in industry and social life just as these stand. Indeed they will raise the question whether any immigration is desirable. Have we not Americans enough out of work to fill every possible job?

But somehow this does not sound truly American. It is not truly American to doubt that our country has a future more brilliant than its past. It is not truly American to assume that there is nothing we can learn from other people.

It was recently reported that in the last five years some fifty new industries had been established in the Montreal district, forty of them by refugees. These are small industries, of course, employing small numbers of men. This does not detract from their social importance. In the interstices among our great industries, our great mercantile organizations, there are to be found everywhere opportunities for small industries, small trades, some of which will grow in time into important factors in our national economic life.

There is no reason why native Americans should not find many of these neglected opportunities. Some in fact are being found every day. But the immigrant who had attained success before he was expelled from his native land and who is bent on rebuilding his position, is likely to search more diligently and persistently for opportunities. Besides, he brings with him many ideas, many techniques, that he can make count directly.

Is it to be supposed that our standards of consumption, admittedly the highest in the world, have reached such a peak that we could not profitably introduce items that our immigrants bring with them? Consider how American dietaries have been improved, to our great benefit, by alien influences' ranging from France to China. Consider the influence of the Italian community upon the general consumption of fresh vegetables. If one had the time one might trace innumerable pleasant advances in our arts of design to the various partly assimilated communities of alien origin.

To sum up, the mass immigration of today will be slower to assimilate completely than the mass immigration of yesterday. Formerly we had only the immigrant himself, a poor, weak individual, to fit into our social economic life, usually at the lowest and simplest level. Now we have immigrants in groups, containing leadership and organizing capacity, that is, a culture. We have to assimilate the immigrant plus his culture. And that plus means two-sided assimilation. We must teach the immigrant our ways, to be sure, but if we wish to profit from him fully, we must also learn his ways, and if these prove good, appropriate them.

We see today in Europe the deadly consequences of the ruthless pursuit of a false ideal of homogeneity. The racial superstition drags with it superstitions of homogeneity of ideas, something that ultimately proves fatal not only to humane ideas, but to fertile ones. There are admittedly risks in ethnic, cultural, religious variety. But these are risks inseparable from the risks of progress.

And let us not forget that the moral splendor that so often shines out in American history owes its existence not to the population types we would choose if prompt but negative assimilation were our goal, but to the types that found no conflict between loyalty to our country and loyalty to themselves, their culture and traditions. Benjamin Franklin did not seek to conform. He maintained steadfastly the free culture and traditions of his own people. That is why he had so much that was unique and valuable to give. Among the thousands whom the new mass immigration promises to bring to us there is an incredibly large proportion who have been expelled from their homelands because they stand for freedom, humanity and individual independence of mind. They will have much to give that will contribute to the future moral greatness of our country.

Repatriation of Greeks, Turks, and Bulgars after the Graeco-Turkish War: 1919-23

By

PHILIP E. MOSELY, PH.D.*

MOST nineteenth and twentieth century thinking about nationalism has been predicated upon the assumption that the existence, or the creation, of a homogeneous national society-state is the highest and inevitable ambition of any ethnic group. This idea, which had unfolded gradually in Western Europe, burst with revolutionary force upon the states and peoples of Eastern Europe. There, prior to the social and political emancipations of the nineteenth century, society and state had for centuries been founded on the principle of caste, not of nationality. Nationality was passive. It was a cluster of culture traits, rather than an activating force. As a consequence of this late-persisting indifference to nationality, Eastern European society has characteristically been multi-ethnic in structure; that is, various ethnic groups have frequently performed different functions and occupied different strata in a highly static society. In these conditions of development lie the origins of the complicated minglings of nationalities which are the delight of ethnographers and the despair of statesmen in dealing with such regions as the Banat, the Bukovina, or pre-1918 Macedonia, to mention only three of the more proverbial instances of ethnically mixed areas.

With the assertion of national consciousness and national ambition, each ethnic nucleus strove to assimilate the population of other ethnic origin within its principal area. Where community of social interest and religious allegiance was strong, it was likely to succeed in this, witness the absorption of the Greeks of Rumania or the Albanians of central Greece. A second and complementary striving of each awakening nationality has been to extend the frontiers of its state to include as

* Associate Professor of History, Cornell University.

many as possible of its fellow-nationals, even at the cost of acquiring large populations of alien stock. The urgings of ethnic "imperialism" have impelled each nation to achieve the frontiers which it regarded as indispensable for the advancement of its national well-being. Success in achieving this ambition has in turn aroused the profound enmity of its dissatisfied neighbors.

In the presence of this seemingly endless *danse macabre* of national egoisms, it is no wonder that people have come more and more to demand that this source of recurrent conflict be eradicated once and for all, even at the price of a grandiose surgical operation. Where history has neglected to create nationally homogeneous states, they can, according to this view, be created by human will. By fixing compromise boundaries somewhere midway between the extreme claims of rival nationalities and then effecting a compulsory exchange of the remaining national minorities, political frontiers can be made to correspond so closely to ethnic frontiers that all justification for continued national "imperialism" can be removed. Then each national state can unite with its neighbors for the advancement of their common regional interests, thus laying the groundwork for regional, European, and ultimately world peace.

This daringly simple proposal for the compulsory exchange of ethnic minorities has taken on a special attraction since the collapse of the European structure which was set up in 1919. The Paris settlement emphasized a quite opposite principle—that of the protection of minorities, ethnic, religious, and linguistic. The Minorities Treaties of 1919-20, while partially rooted in earlier international instruments, were unique in that they were intended to establish a substantial minimum of guaranteed rights for an unprecedented number of people. From the beginning the Minorities Treaties suffered from a number of external obstacles and internal contradictions. One chief handicap was the different light in which they were regarded by the minority and majority nationalities. The majority nationalities felt that the treaties were designed merely to ease the transition to the new regime, and refused to accept them as perpetual restrictions on their national sovereignty. In their zeal to redress the balance against their previous oppressors, the majority nationalities resented the existence of unilateral obligations which in some measure hampered them in promoting the political and social progress of their own peoples. The minorities, on the other hand, usually regarded the treaties as instruments for perpetuating their claims to fresh territorial changes, rather than as the basis of a permanent settlement, and in the meantime they used them, as often as not, to blackmail the majority nationalities into leaving untouched as many as possible of their acquired social and other advantages. This contradiction in understanding and applying the Minorities Treaties was a principal factor in the failure of the treaties to achieve their fundamental purpose, which was that of effecting a genuine reconciliation between the minority and majority nationalities within the newly created or enlarged states.

The breakdown of the post-1918 system of minority protection has brought to more favorable attention the opposite principle, that of the compulsory exchange of national minorities. When first applied on a large scale, in the compulsory repatriation of the Greek and Turkish minorities after 1922, this principle was accepted against the strenuous opposition of the populations directly affected and over the horrified protests of the western world. Despite its inauspicious origins, the Graeco-Turkish settlement has since come to be regarded as a very beneficial, if drastic, solution of what had appeared to be an insoluble nationality problem. Since then, generalizing from this successful application of the principle of compulsory exchange, statesmen and publicists have urged that it be applied on a broad scale, and in many parts of Europe, as a way out of the blind-alley of perpetual national conflict and war.

Since the outbreak of the present European war several compulsory exchanges or repatriations of minorities have actually taken place. Following Hitler's Reichstag speech of October 6, 1939, the German government signed repatriation agreements with Esthonia, Latvia, Italy, and the Soviet Union. By a curious paradox, Hitler has been repatriating German minorities from the territories, actual or promised, of his allies, while he has been waging a war allegedly undertaken to protect another German minority, in Poland. By the end of 1939 considerable transfers of population had taken place; 16,000 Germans had left Esthonia; 62,000, Latvia. In northern Italy, of

268,000 Germans, 185,000, or 69 percent, had elected to emigrate to Germany within a two-year period.

The process of reshuffling populations received additional impetus from the German-Soviet partition of Poland. By January 31, 1940, 118,000 Germans had been repatriated from Soviet-occupied Poland, and an unspecified number of Ukrainians and White Russians had been transferred from the German to the Soviet sphere. Simultaneously, some five to six million Poles were driven out of Pomorze, Poznan, and Upper Silesia into rump-Poland, or the Government-General. In late 1939 the Nazi government had plans under way to create a purely Jewish "reservation" around Lublin by driving out the Polish inhabitants and replacing them with about two and a half million Jews from Germany, Austria, Czechoslovakia, and western Poland; this project has been left in abeyance, not because of its barbarous character, but because of the economic and hygienic dangers to which it would subject the entire German-occupied area. The Soviet seizure of Bessarabia and northern Bukovina in June, 1940, was followed by arrangements for the evacuation of about 120,000 Germans to the Reich. The Rumanian-Bulgarian agreement of September 7, 1940, for the return of southern Dobruja to Bulgaria, provided also for the compulsory exchange of their respective minorities. On the other hand, the Rumanian-Hungarian agreement for the partition of Transylvania, which was dictated by the Axis Powers on August 30, 1940, made no provision for the compulsory exchange of minorities; by this accession Hungary acquired between three and four times as many Rumanians as there were Magyars left within the truncated Rumanian state, and under these conditions an exchange of minorities was hardly feasible.

Although forced migrations of religious, social, and political minorities have occurred time and again in the past, the Graeco-Turkish exchange of minorities after 1922 struck the imagination of the world with a peculiar force. To be sure, nearly every territorial change in the Balkans has been followed by more or less compulsory transfers of population, but the Greek exodus from Asia Minor made a lasting impression because of the tragic plight of the refugees, because of the large numbers involved, and also because of the dramatic mustering of international assistance to save the lives of the victims and to resettle them in their new homes.[1] After the collapse of the Greek army before a resurgent Turkey, the entire Greek population of Asia Minor was faced with the choice of flight or annihilation. In all, from 1912 to 1924, between 1,300,000 and 1,500,000 Greeks fled to European Greece; to make room for them, about 400,000 Turks were removed from Greek Macedonia to Anatolia. The terms of the exchange were embodied in the Repatriation Convention signed by Greece and Turkey in 1923, as a supplement to the Treaty of Lausanne.

One result of the exchange has been to change drastically the ethnic character of several important areas. Greek Macedonia, in which the Greeks were in 1912 only 42.6 percent of the population, became 83.3 percent Greek by 1924, while Anatolia became almost purely Turkish. As a result of a more complicated series of exchanges involving Greece, Bulgaria, and Turkey, Western Thrace changed from 36.7 percent Greek in 1912 to 62.1 percent in 1924, while Eastern Thrace, which was restored to Turkey by the Treaty of Lausanne, changed from 39.1 percent Moslem in 1912 to 95 percent Turkish in 1924.[2] As a result of the exchanges, regions which formerly were hotly contested between two or even more nationalities have become nationally homogeneous, or very nearly so. The claims of both Greece and Turkey to their present territories have been correspondingly strengthened. By contrast, Greek Epirus or Qamuria, where the Albanians, even the Moslem Albanians, were exempted from the provisions of exchange, is a danger-zone today (September, 1940).

Even after the exchange of population between Greece and Turkey was completed in 1924, the problem of securing to the Greek refugees some compensation for their abandoned property seemed likely to embitter the relations between the two states for an indefinite period. Through Venizelos' statesmanlike gesture the controversy was ended by a treaty of De-

[1] See the *Quarterly Reports of the Refugee Settlement Commission* of the League of Nations (Nos. 1-27, Geneva); Charles B. Eddy, *Greece and the Greek refugees* (London, 1931); Stephen P. Ladas, *The exchange of minorities; Bulgaria, Greece, and Turkey* (New York, 1932). For the Graeco-Bulgar exchange see André Wurfbain, *L'échange gréco-bulgare des minorités ethniques* (Lausanne, 1930).

[2] The best available analysis of statistics for these areas is that of A. A. Pallis, "Racial migrations in the Balkans during the years 1912-1924," *The Geographical Journal*, vol. xlvi (1925), pp. 315-331.

cember 1930 in which the two governments canceled their claims and wiped the slate clean. Since then the two states have become firm friends. They have met several international crises in close coöperation. Between 1934 and 1940 they worked together in promoting the Balkan Entente. In addition to these political gains each country has derived certain social and economic advantages from the exchange. Greece has become self-sufficient in wheat, and is now a large producer of tobacco. Several Anatolian industries, such as the carpet-making of Brusa, have been transferred to Greece. While Turkey underwent a great immediate loss through the expulsion of a large part of its commercial and peasant population, it has since developed more numerous business and professional classes of Turkish stock than it had previously possessed.

One unforeseen advantage which Greece derived from the settlement of the refugees was that it facilitated—indeed, it made imperative—a large-scale work of economic and social reconstruction. A considerably larger population had now to be supported from the same supply of land, a supply which could be enlarged only slightly by reclamation projects. The refugees had to be made self-supporting as quickly as possible, for they were destitute and starving; the Greek state itself was completely exhausted after twelve years of war. The health of the refugees had to be restored and safeguarded. They needed to recover hope and an incentive to work and save. They had to be integrated into their new communities. All these needs made imperative the development of rural reconstruction along lines and on a scale previously unknown in the Balkans. In meeting this problem several agencies made notable contributions, particularly, the Greek government, the League of Nations, the Rockefeller Foundation, and the Near East Relief, later the Near East Foundation. Probably the most novel and fruitful experiment made was that undertaken by the Near East Foundation in 1929.[3] Through trial and error an effective program of rural improvement was gradually evolved. In its

[3] Part of the information on which this part of the article is based was graciously placed at the disposal of the author by Dr. Harold B. Allen, who is writing an account of the reconstruction work in Greek Macedonia. Dr. Allen was Educational Director of the Caucasus area of the Near East Relief, 1926-30, and Director of Education for the Near East Foundation, 1930-38; since 1938 President of the National Farm School, Bucks County, Pennsylvania. Dr. Allen is not responsible for any opinions expressed by the author.

final form, each of eight farm experts became responsible for agricultural and, later, community improvement in a group of six villages. By contrast, it should be noted that under the Greek Ministry of Agriculture each farm agent had charge of about 250 villages, and hence could make no effective contribution to solving their problems. Because of the success of the experiment, the Greek government in 1937 revised its program of rural service, and is building up its agricultural program as fast as trained leaders can be provided. Beginning in 1931, the Foundation made several experiments in promoting home welfare work in the villages. The program which was worked out over several years was remarkably successful in improving sanitation, child-training, and family-care, and is now used as a basis for training home economics agents for work throughout the country. The Foundation also worked out programs for sanitation and community recreation. From the refugee villages the movement has spread to the native settlements, and it is hoped ultimately to extend it to the entire country. The methods and programs worked out in Greek Macedonia are also exerting a profound influence on the development of rural reconstruction throughout the Balkans and the Near East. Without the immediate and desperate need created by the influx of refugees, this fruitful program might never have been undertaken. If subsequent exchanges of minorities are followed up with similar programs of social reconstruction, the immediate losses caused by the repatriation will be lessened, and the long-run effects may be highly advantageous.

The reconstruction program in Greek Macedonia was, to be sure, undertaken as a direct consequence of the refugee influx, but there is no necessary connection between the repatriation of minorities and rural reconstruction. Remaking the life and work of the village is a pressing need today in every peasant country, and many efforts are being made to cope with it. In Bulgaria this tremendous task has been tackled from several sides, and with much success, without its being tied up with the refugee problem. A less consistent, but very interesting effort has been made in Rumania, through the Prince Carol Foundation and the "cultural centers" which have been set up in about fifteen hundred villages. The Croat People's Party has likewise carried on an extensive program of rural improvement since just before the World War of 1914. Similar programs are being worked out in Albania and Turkey, in Syria, Iraq, Cyprus, and Palestine. In the case of Greek Macedonia the influx of refugees meant that experiments in social reconstruction could be undertaken at a time when the peasants' resistance to innovation was at a low ebb; but despite the greater initial repugnance to change which is found in long-settled villages, results similar to those achieved among the refugees can be and are being brought about in several parts of the world, without subjecting the population to the disaster of compulsory repatriation.

Despite the beneficial consequences which developed somewhat accidentally from the Graeco-Turkish exchange, this reshuffling of populations was accompanied by several unfavorable features which are likely to be repeated in later exchanges. In the first place, the uprooting of the minorities meant that they had been subjected to extremely severe and prolonged oppression. Only when they were threatened with immediate physical annihilation, and, in part, subjected to it, were the Greeks of Anatolia willing to abandon their ancestral homes and flee to Greece. In the second place, the word "exchange" is rather a misnomer when applied to the Greek exodus, since over three times as many Greeks as Turks were involved in the process of exchange. Finally, it is impossible to assess the economic and social values which were lost in the exchange. The Graeco-Turkish experience showed that it is all but impossible to provide compensation for the physical properties left behind by the refugees, not to mention compensation for the social costs involved in uprooting and resettling a large population.

In addition to these disadvantages, it must not be forgotten that an exchange of minorities does not, of and by itself, stabilize international frontiers. Other factors are of equal, or greater, importance. In the case of Greece and Turkey, the two countries since 1923 have had only a very short stretch of common frontier, and each country has much longer and more exposed frontiers with its other neighbors. During the past decade the new-found friendship between Greece and Turkey has been based as much on their common desire to keep Bulgaria isolated and, since 1935, on their growing dread of Italian aggression, as on the elimination of the minority problem. The fact that such an exchange does not in itself stabilize frontiers is illustrated by the results of the Graeco-Bulgarian exchange.

Although the Bulgarians are now only a small minority (7.5 percent, as of 1924) in Western Thrace, they still lay claim to all or part of this province on strategic and economic grounds. Although the question of southern Dobruja has now been settled to its own satisfaction, Bulgaria has already opened a new campaign for the recovery of Western Thrace.

Frontier claims are as often based on strategic, economic, and historical factors as on ethnic distribution. The assumption that a general cancelling out of ethnic claims through the compulsory exchange of minorities would remove the principal source of conflict in Europe does not stand up under close scrutiny. Stabilization of frontiers in Europe may be achieved through an effective system of collective security, or through the control of the entire continent by a dominant state. If such stability were once assured, it would be a matter of relatively minor importance whether ethnic minorities remained in their present homes, or whether they were repatriated to their ethnic homelands. Under stabilized conditions, minorities would no longer be so serious a source of strife; both national states and national minorities might well learn to live together if the hope, or the fear, of perpetual territorial changes were removed.

If the compulsory exchange of national minorities becomes a normal accompaniment of territorial change, and is not accomplished as part of a general process of political stabilization, the results will be tragic. If each change of frontier posts is followed by wholesale shiftings of population, the sufferings of the frontier peoples and of the countries affected will be multiplied many times over. Such repeated and large-scale repatriations would lower the economic and cultural standards of European life. Finally, the general acceptance of the principle of compulsory exchange would completely destroy whatever protection minorities have enjoyed till now. A state which showed no mercy to its minorities would benefit by its own policy of ruthlessness, while one which displayed some respect for minority rights would be penalized by the persistence of irredentist claims promoted by its neighbors.

Despite these shortcomings and dangers, the principle of compulsory exchange is being extended, and is likely to be extended still further. It is being thrust to the fore by the increasing interference of the state in the lives of its citizens. As long as the state plays a small part in the lives of its subjects and confines its activities mainly to the collection of taxes and the defense of its boundaries, ethnic minorities survive, and may even prosper. But as the state demands more types of services from its citizens and in turn fulfils increasingly elaborate functions in developing the economic, social, and cultural life of its people, the position of an ethnic minority becomes more and more difficult. At moments of great political tension that position may be a tragic one. Because of the growing impact of the state on the lives of its citizens it may well be that both ethnic minorities and ethnic majorities will eventually be driven to accept the principle of the compulsory exchange of national minorities as an escape from the continuing havoc of mutual hate and common ruin.

Refugees in the Americas

By

WILLIAM HABER, Ph.D.*

THE magnitude of the world refugee problem cannot be fully measured until the outcome of the present conflict in Europe is determined. Estimates of the number of refugees for whom emigration opportunities must be found have changed almost monthly as the Nazi conquest and the economic ravages of war affect new areas. Where hundreds of thousands were involved a few months ago, millions of men, women and children are concerned today. And it is unlikely that the conclusion of hostilities will materially contract the size of this problem.

Whoever is the victor in the tragic struggle, millions of people will be forced to emigrate. Economic duress, a desire to keep alive political convictions, anti-racial legislation or, as in the case of hundreds of thousands of men and women—mere flight from the firing squad or the concentration camp—all these factors will, in addition to the unprecedented economic adjustments which must be made after the war's end, influence the magnitude of the world refugee problem. It now seems certain that when President Roosevelt, in addressing the Intergovernmental Committee on Refugees in the fall of 1939, declared that with the cessation of hostilities the world might be concerned with as many as ten million refugees, he was not overstating the size of the problem.

Immigration from Europe to the New World is of deep historical significance. The countries of North and South America were settled by Europeans. In the century between 1820 and 1920 the United States alone received over 34,000,000 immigrants from Europe. And the countries of South America have also been peopled by the immigrant millions from Italy, Spain and Portugal, Germany and other lands.

The present problem, however, differs from the traditional

* Professor of Economics, University of Michigan; Former Executive Director, National Refugee Service, Inc.

immigration in several respects. To a larger extent than ever before, this is "forced" migration; it is also mass migration. It is concerned not only with thousands of individuals who naturally seek more ample economic opportunities in newer countries, but with tens of thousands who must flee. Many, if not most of these, do not possess the necessary funds for transportation or the wherewithal to begin economic life anew. In addition, immigration which takes place under pressure, and often in defiance of ordinary economic motives, is concerned with people who must emigrate because their condition is desperate and not because of their chances of making good in the receiving country. Ordinarily immigrants do not go to places where trade may be had and the standard of living is falling— Shanghai, now harboring some thousands of European refugees, is an example of such a forced refuge; nor do they select countries where the conditions are unfavorable and where the essentials of life have to be secured by hard pioneering. The very word "refugee" suggests that the individual, in moving to another country, "is not actuated so much by the attraction of the place to which he is going as by grim necessity of getting away from where he is."[1]

These aspects of the problem are especially significant, for many areas of the world which can afford a liberal immigration policy (South American countries and Canada for example) seek primarily immigrants who are able to work on land, who have some capital, or possess specific mechanical or technical skills. These requirements do not, in general, characterize the refugees of recent years, nor are they indicative particularly of the millions who will be involved in the after-war readjustments.

The refugee settlements that have taken place in the New World in recent years have largely been inspired and financed by private efforts. It has become increasingly evident, however, that the final settlement of many thousands of refugees uprooted by the war and the Nazi terror cannot be accomplished by relying on private efforts alone. A concerted policy of many governments is necessary if colonization or settlement schemes are to be successful. There are serious financial considerations quite beyond the scope of private subscriptions. There are other difficulties largely revolving around the central problem:

[1] Sir John Hope Simpson, *Refugees—A Review of the Situation since September 1938*, p. 9.

In what country or countries are large scale colonization schemes possible? Are such schemes practical, particularly in relation to the known occupational qualifications of the emigrating group? What countries are in need of population expansion and can utilize the training and experience of the men and women who are refugees?

The tremendous pressure for emigration now prevailing in Europe suggests, even in advance of the answer to these questions, certain immediate steps which appear to be necessary. Among these, the most important is "adequate provision for a temporary refuge." The subjugation of practically all continental countries by the German military machine has removed every haven which before the outbreak of the war provided temporary refuge for those in flight from Central Europe. Many of these have been trapped again. Others have had to flee for the second, third or perhaps fourth time, only to find that most avenues of escape have been blocked.

In addition to the need for a temporary haven of refuge there is urgent need for pressing on with studies of possible areas of immigration in the Western Hemisphere and elsewhere. In view of the size and complicated nature of the problem there is need for the creation of a clearing center for labor and skills available in the group awaiting emigration. "There is an artificially created pool of highly trained professional persons; of business men with knowledge of foreign markets; of manufacturers and technicians, and workmen in a great variety of industries, notably in those branches where Central Europe has had a practical monopoly or has been in the first rank."[2] Here are skills and other technical resources which offer an opportunity for definite enrichment to the newer countries.

II

Refugees who have come to the United States since 1933 are making a relatively rapid adjustment to the economic and social requirements of their new home. Their number is not large, in fact, between 1933 and 1938 the quota allowed by our immigration laws was never filled, even from the Central European countries. The total number of permanent visa immi-

[2] *Ibid.*, p. 9.

grants who entered the United States during the entire period 1933 to 1941, who may be classified as refugees, is probably less than 175,000.[3]

When this number is considered in relation to a total U. S. population of over 130,000,000 any adverse effect that it might possibly have on our national economy must be set aside as inconsequential. Admittedly a considerable number of émigrés come with challenging problems of social and economic adjustment. But at the same time others bring with them skills and potentialities for service which more than compensate. It may be difficult to find an American use for the experience and knowledge of a German banker or a Czech lawyer. But the effort is repaid a thousandfold by the presence of a Thomas Mann, Toscanini, Lotte Lehman, Albert Einstein, Maurice Maeterlinck, Heinrich Bruening, Max Reinhardt, and Bruno Walter, to name just a few of the outstanding refugees whose old-world careers have suffered no interruption.

Refugees who have come to the United States are of all types. There are scholars and scientists, musicians, doctors and dentists, ministers and engineers, former merchants and tradesmen, store clerks, salesmen, skilled mechanics and laborers. And some are just children.

The children, together with the men who are too old to work and the women who will remain at home constitute about 55 percent of the total émigré group in the United States. Of the balance, nearly 8 percent are in the professional ranks; 12 percent are skilled workers; 18 percent were identified with commercial organizations as managers or employees; domestic workers compose 4 percent, and less than 1 percent have an agricultural background.

The skilled craftsmen, representing 12 percent of the total, present no adjustment problem. If anything, there is a shortage in the United States of watchmakers, glass workers, machinists, potters, fine tool workers, and toy makers. Virtually all refugees having such qualifications have had early placement in industry.

One of the most worthwhile developments arising out of the

[3] Refugee Emigration from the European continent to the United States as well as to other nations has been restricted considerably in 1941 as a result of the Nazi occupation of nearly the entire continent. United States immigration regulations were also revised in 1941 and will probably result in increasing difficulties to immigrants desiring admission to the U. S.

refugee migration has been the establishment of small mercantile and manufacturing concerns producing, for the most part,
articles previously imported. Many of these concerns were
started by former entrepreneurs or commercial employees who
came to the United States between 1933 and 1938 and were able
to salvage some economic resources. A number were able to
secure financial backing on this side. As previous generations
of immigrants brought with them to America new ideas, new
products, and new skills, so this refugee group has created
jobs for American labor through the production of skis, toys,
wallets, gloves, German cakes and confectioneries, photographic
supplies, glassware, chinaware, and many other commodities.
A sample survey conducted by the National Refugee Service
in 1939 examined 303 business enterprises initiated by recent
newcomers. Two factors were especially significant: In almost
all instances, the concerns were producing goods of a non-
competitive character, and 75 percent of the workers employed
were native Americans. The capital investments in these businesses varied from insignificant sums to amounts over $100,000,
and in four cases the annual production of the company was
in excess of $200,000. Following are brief accounts of a few
of the new refugee industries:

A two-hundred-and-fifty-year-old firm was moved from Prague to
New York City in 1937. It manufactures glass products formerly
imported from Czechoslovakia. This firm has also developed a new
photo-chemical process for glass printing.

A refugee patent holder, producing a hot wax carbonizing process, has established a business with an annual gross income of over
$100,000.

Filtermass, 94% of which was previously imported from Germany
by the American domestic brewing industry, is now being manufactured by two refugee firms in this country. Ten American workers and two refugees are employed in this new industry, which has
a total capital of about $25,000.

It would be erroneous to conclude from the foregoing that
all refugees who have reached our shores are finding a satisfactory economic adjustment. The road is a long one, and, especially for those who have lost considerable status in the process,
it is a road fraught with disappointments. Many of the émigrés
formerly engaged in business abroad have presented difficult
placement problems. American business methods are new to

them. Inability to speak English, lack of capital, and factors of age and personality still further complicate the problem.

Perhaps the chief limiting factor has been their lack of training for any but their own work. This is one of the most formidable challenges presented by the refugee population. It is no easy matter to devise and carry out an effective method of retraining an ex-banker. A program for vocational retraining and readjustment is under way for some of the commercial group, but up to now the number affected has been relatively small. Many of the former merchants and storekeepers are worrying along in jobs generally not related to their European experience.

The need for re-thinking one's life work is especially poignant in the case of European lawyers, who face a situation which even the hardiest of them, in possession of the necessary funds, can rarely have the temerity to essay. The entire body of German law is totally different from our own. The lawyer must attend an American law school, graduate, and pass his bar examinations. Even after this has been accomplished, he must wait to become a citizen before he is allowed to practise. Actors and singers have a language handicap to overcome, although a few very successful adjustments have been made. The same is true to an even greater degree of journalists.

Many teachers and scholars in the arts, and in the social and physical sciences, banished from their German and Italian university posts, have come to the United States to carry on their work. Thanks to the efforts of the Emergency Committee in Aid of Displaced Foreign Scholars, research and other positions have been located for many of these refugees on the faculties of many of our institutions of higher learning, notably in the smaller colleges. The "University in Exile" of the New School for Social Research in New York has absorbed a number. Refugee scientists in the field of medicine have been aided in their attempts to resume their research and teaching by the Emergency Committee in Aid of Displaced Foreign Medical Scientists. But, on the whole, the total number placed represents only a small percentage of the group.

The situation with respect to refugee physicians has been aired in the medical journals and in several other publications, but a further statement of the problem may be in order. From the knowledge that "there are at least 2,000 opportunities for practice of which American physicians have not availed them-selves,"[4] one might conclude that the services of émigré physicians could be utilized in certain rural districts. But the reality confronting the refugee doctor is that in forty-four states, statutory provisions or administrative regulations prevent him from entering practice. In twenty-eight states, for example, a practicing doctor must be a citizen, regardless of his other qualifications. The same obstacles prevent refugee doctors from filling any but a few of the hundreds of available internships in approved hospitals which remain unfilled from American medical schools.

Largely through the efforts of the National Committee for Resettlement of Foreign Physicians, about 1,000 of the total of 2,500 refugee physicians now in this country have been settled in practice in a number of large cities and rural communities. The Committee hopes to be able to place the greater part of the others, but the procedure is arduous, long and expensive, and in the light of diminishing placement opportunities attempts are being made to divert to other fields those least likely to pass their examinations. It can well be understood that this is a difficult decision for a group of physicians to arrive at and for the Committee to transmit to one of their number. But the Committee feels, especially in the case of those who are receiving cash assistance from one of the refugee-aid agencies, that it is senseless to prolong, beyond a certain point, the fiction that a man will some day reënter practice, when all known evidence leads to the contrary conclusion.

The percentage of all refugees given financial assistance by the privately financed refugee organizations is small, though somewhat higher than it was in the earlier years of the immigration when those fleeing Europe were able to take with them a greater proportion of their savings. Among those receiving aid are visitors from Germany, France, Poland and other countries who were trapped in the United States when war broke out. The bulk of the refugees, however, are either self-supporting or receiving financial aid from their affidavit signers, and relatives, and their contact with the agencies is for other kinds of service.

A visit to the New York offices of the American Committee

[4] David L. Edsall, "The Emigré Physician in American Medicine," *Journal of the American Medical Association*, March 23, 1940.

for Christian Refugees, the American Friends Service Committee, the Catholic Committee for Aid of Refugees from Germany, and the National Refugee Service—the main refugee-aid agencies—will reveal a variety of services given by professional staffs and designed to aid in the economic and social orientation of refugees who have come to the United States. The largest organization is maintained by the National Refugee Service, representing the majority of those refugees who have come. This agency serves refugees in the areas of migration, employment, temporary relief and case work service, resettlement, and social and cultural adjustment.

The migration service is concerned with immigration problems of refugees all over the world who are destined for or seek entry into the United States, and provides information and advice for their relatives and friends in this country.

The employment service functions in a manner similar to others operated by private social agencies, endeavors to evaluate émigrés on the basis of their work experience abroad and to place them, insofar as possible, in non-competitive employment. This service includes a retraining program to expedite placement of those employable and needy refugees whose skills brought from abroad have no immediate market in the United States. Working closely with the employment department are a group of special committees set up to advise and place agriculturists, ministers, musicians, physicians and others. There is also a self-support unit which gives limited capital loans to refugees who have a sound business plan.

Financial assistance is given to refugees whose affiants have been unable to live up to their promises of support, and offer skilled family case work service.

The Social and Cultural Division of the National Refugee Service serves as a clearing house and information center for refugees on the social, religious and educational resources available for their use in the community, including referral to free English classes.

Resettlement is the agency's primary objective because it offers to the refugee his best chance for constructive adjustment to the American way of life. Immigrants have always piled up in New York. The melting pot is an arresting conception—but unfortunately one that has often existed in theory rather than in fact. In the case of refugees, New York has still another fatal attraction, in that as the main port of entry it offers them their first tangible evidence of security. This hesitancy to leave the city where their relatives or friends may be located is understandable, even though it may be false security so far as long term economic adjustment is concerned.

In the past seven years many refugees have found their way to other cities where relatives or friends were living, or have even ventured out on their own. But the number in New York has continued to increase. For a time, sporadic efforts to resettle individual families were made by the agency, but this did not result in any considerable volume. As a consequence, the formation of local refugee committees in large, medium-size, and small cities throughout the United States was initiated as the first step in a planned resettlement policy. In a period of two years over 500 committees were organized all over the country. Each of these committees, depending on the size of the community and the kind of resources available, agrees to a self-imposed monthly quota of refugees. In accordance with the agreement made the national organization sends out family units, provided with transportation costs and temporary living expenses where the family does not have its own funds. The local committee endeavors to find work for the bread-winner of the family, and if this is not accomplished assumes responsibility for the family's support until such time as it becomes self-supporting. To facilitate the exploration of community resources and follow-up once the refugee reaches the community of his destination, the country has been divided into well-defined regions which operate as part of the national program. Through the functioning of a field-staff efforts are made to provide the community with émigrés whose personality, background and vocational skills seem adaptable to the town in question.

The total number of individuals resettled in 1939, the first year when resettlement was offered as the agency's "main chance," was close to 4,000. During 1940 the number resettled out of New York was nearly 6,000 despite the fact that immigration at the port of New York has slowed down considerably in recent months. With the recent arrival of small numbers of refugees at West Coast ports, and at Boston and Miami, a certain amount of resettlement has been effected directly from those centers, and this too has been a factor in relieving the situation in New York.

Naturally enough, not all families resettled have taken root as yet in their new surroundings. But on the basis of the evidence we have to date, the period of economic and social assimilation is much shorter in the country at large than it is in New York City. Experience indicates that there is relatively greater possibility of making a fresh start outside of New York, as opposed to the limited existence led by most refugees who are trying to gain a foothold in the big city.

III

The possibilities of large-scale immigration to South American countries have long been considered by those seeking a partial solution for the refugee problem. Latin America provides a hope for those eager to relieve the distress of millions suffering in the devastated areas of Europe. The countries composing it are rich in natural resources, relatively undeveloped commercially, industrially and agriculturally, and underpopulated. Most of the South American nations have always lacked the manpower and the capital to exploit their resources. Accordingly, for a long time immigration was neither hindered nor restricted.

After 1933 a considerable number of refugees—both from Germany and the surrounding European countries in which they had taken temporary refuge—emigrated to the Latin American republics. The total number of refugees in all these countries at the present time is estimated at 125,000. During the past few years the South American countries have restricted immigration. In doing so, some of the smaller countries have sought to limit immigration to prospective farmers—a policy dictated by the great need for increased agricultural productivity. For despite their potentialities for economic self-sufficiency many of these countries have to import foodstuffs. The bulk of the refugee migration since 1933 has consisted of urban settlers rather than farm workers. The present immigrants do not possess the necessary capital or occupational experience for farm work, and the methods of the commercial settlement companies, which have played an important role in the previous colonization, are not applicable to the present problem. The native population consequently has developed a resentful attitude toward these newcomers who do not produce, but as consumers are considered responsible for the rise in the price of foodstuffs.

The consequence is that today the traditional open door has been almost entirely shut to refugee immigrants. Where the door remains open and some flexibility in policy prevails, there are serious political and social obstacles to admission. Despite these factors, however, a considerable number of immigrants still gain entrance into Latin American countries. Argentina and Brazil continue to admit some; Ecuador has shown itself to be hospitable. The possibilities of new immigration into British and Dutch Guiana and to British Honduras have been given sympathetic interest. Many technical obstacles prevail, however, and there is little immediate prospect for extensive settlement in these areas. A promising project for the settlement of refugees has been launched under favorable auspices in the Dominican Republic, although the number settled is as yet small. Mexico and Chile have admitted substantial numbers of Spanish Republican as well as Central European refugees and it is anticipated that others will be brought in and settled on the land. The problems involved in refugee immigration and adaptation are not simple. The solution is complicated by the current conflicts and fears which characterize national policy everywhere. Nations are cautious; minority groups are suspect.

As in other countries, political and national considerations have influenced the immigration policy of South American countries. Out of the large German and Italian migrations in earlier years have grown compact foreign colonies, many with strong loyalties to their countries of origin as well as to their lands of adoption. The relatively conspicuous Jewish immigration since 1938 has naturally evoked some expressions of nationalistic character. These have been inspired and intensified by Nazi propaganda.

Notwithstanding the fears—expressed and unexpressed—it may well be questioned whether there is any real danger that refugee immigration to South America will provide the subversive elements inimical to the interests of the receiving countries. So-called fifth column activity—a genuine threat to the internal security of many nations—does not originate or find its support from the group which has been fleeing for its very life from the totalitarian forces in ruthless control of Central Europe. The Nazis have no doubt sought to send abroad a number of their own agents in the guise of refugees, and eternal vigilance is necessary on the part of nations. Nevertheless, the great bulk of the refugees are neither Nazis nor preachers of Nazi doctrines. This is not a careless observation but one made after careful thought and extensive contact with the refugee problem. It applies to the United States as well as to South America. All who are interested in ferreting out the fifth columnists will make a dangerous error in assuming that a source of this treasonable danger to national security is to be found among the refugees, or, for that matter, to any considerable degree among the alien population in the United States. In a statement made July 7, in which he cautioned against the unjust condemnation of aliens, Solicitor-General Francis Biddle said, "I think there is little doubt that most of the several million aliens in the United States are people who believe sincerely in the principles of American democracy."

Some students have questioned whether the South American republics have the potential possibilities for large-scale immigration that seem apparent on the surface. Brazil's enormous expanse, it has been stated, could support a population of over 375,000,000. Yet according to Isaiah Bowman, writing of the pre-refugee immigration, there has always been a high return of Brazilian immigrants to their mother country, amounting to 48 percent in the State of Sao Paulo alone. Mr. Bowman, writing in 1937, concludes that "Brazil has enormous possibilities of expansion of cultivable land, but its low technological level and its loose political organization preclude firm central guidance of the agencies that might provide rational settlement schemes in the broad and diversified territories where settlers have gone in recent years."[5] After fifty years of large-scale immigration "Brazil, alone among the great immigration countries has still an enormous area of undeveloped land of great fertility, situated in zones in which the European can easily become acclimatized."[6]

Whatever may have been true in the past, many observers believe South America's present immigration policy to be short-

[5] *Limits of Land Resettlement* (Council on Foreign Relations).
[6] *Ibid.*

sighted in view of changed world economic conditions. The resources of some South American countries can support a population several times the present size. An increase in population would permit a more effectual organization of the national economy—particularly of transportation, trade, health, and other public services. A more liberal immigration policy would speed the process materially.

That the fulfillment of the potentialities of South America can ever be brought about by its native population without the infiltration of additional Europeans is at least highly debatable. Definite advantages would accrue from increased immigration, some of which are discernible even in the limited amount that has taken place to date. Additional population would make the continent's 16,000 miles of virtually unprotected coastline that much less vulnerable from the viewpoint of defense. The vocational aptitude, cultural advancement and relatively high living standards of the European group would greatly enrich the social and economic level of the nations. This has in fact been recognized by a number of the South American countries.

The refugees who have come to South America during the past several years have, to a great extent, been absorbed by industry and commerce. They have found work in the enterprises owned by the native white population or have established small businesses of their own, which, as in the United States, have provided employment for the native population and for other refugees. Successfully operated small industries and trades bear witness to their enterprise.

Despite the effect of the vicious anti-refugee propaganda dispensed by the Nazi elements in South America—propaganda which in some measure has been responsible for the decrease in immigration possibilities—the influx of refugees in recent years has not brought about any serious political complications.

IV

Finally, it may be suggested that the concept of hemispheric defense may well include the possibility of a hemispheric immigration policy. This hemisphere, from Alaska to the tip of South America, not forgetting the many islands in the Atlantic and the Pacific, still possesses greater opportunities for population expansion and for exploitation of untouched resources than any similar area on the face of the globe.

There is little question that the attitude of the United States towards immigration, and towards the immigrants coming to our shores will greatly influence, perhaps even determine, the policies of other nations in this hemisphere. To the extent that we as a people and as a government maintain a liberal, non-discriminatory policy towards the refugee in this country, we will be offsetting the fears of other countries in the hemisphere.

The intelligent manner in which registration of aliens has been carried on in the United States is very much in line with the American tradition of fair play to all its residents. Our policy, based on the proposition that immigrants are assets rather than liabilities, will do much to reaffirm and strengthen the treasured tradition of providing a haven of refuge which is our heritage. And the continuance of a sensible and reasonably liberal immigration policy in the United States will contribute to the creation of a similar attitude among our good neighbors to the north and south.